Donald Harvey Tippet

San Francisco

1957

THE COMING WORLD CIVILIZATION

WILLIAM ERNEST HOCKING

THE COMING
WORLD
CIVILIZATION

HARPER & BROTHERS PUBLISHERS NEW YORK

To

JOHN WAUGH SCOTT

of Glasgow and Cardiff

who has seen from afar
and has aided
the arriving civitas mundi

UT JAM UNIVERSUS HIC MUNDUS
UNA CIVITAS SIT
COMMUNIS DEORUM ATQUE HOMINUM
EXISTIMANDA

Cicero, *De Legibus*, 1, 7

CONTENTS

ENVOI

In the ripeness of years I am inclined to a moment of prophecy. I wish to discern what character our civilizations, now unsteadily merging into a single world civilization, are destined to take in the foreseeable future, assuming that we have a foreseeable future. And what can be deciphered of the roles to be carried by state and church, our two institutional interpreters of total human nature. Are two needed, the one national, the other world-wide? Are they to be independent? Is there at the core of our present era of wrath and insecurity an impulse toward a humane order, measurably free from want and fear, in which church or state or both might wither away?

As foreview requires, I shall have in mind past movements of the civilizations eastern and western. There will be frequent reference to the views of Arnold Toynbee who, as no other historian of our time, has made salient the major issues that emerge in interpreting the interaction of civilizations, and in reading the portent of historical change. Prominent among these issues is that of the significance of the secularization of modern life, the extrusion of religion, not wholly but from omnicompetence, in science, law and politics, business, education, the fine arts.

Not in opposition to Toynbee, but in some contrast with him, I shall regard that secularization as an advance, having a certain necessity and therefore a degree of permanence. Appearing first in the western world, it took shape as a repudiation-in-extent of the claims of western

religion over the major arts of life. Yet, as I read the event,
it was less a rejection than a paradoxical offspring of
Christianity. And further, the partial de-Christianization
of the West brought about by the various secular movements is destined to work not only to the net advantage
of the West, but also to that of a reconceived Christianity.
While curing western arts of a dependent Christianism, it
has helped to cure Christianity of a hampering westernism, revealing to each its latent universality, and stripping
both for the severe labors of world functions lying before
whatever is universal in art or science or law or religion,
and whatever can become universal.

At the same time, this advance, through misunderstand-
ing its own nature—as is common with revolutionary
passages of thought—has brought a deep-seated malaise
from which we now suffer. I concur with Toynbee that
among other matters the spirit of individual liberty, in
which so much of the greatness of modernity is vested, is
touched with disease. Diagnosis of the malady in all its
aspects becomes an essential part of any judgment of the
prospects for civilization. And diagnoses are now widely
being offered, many valuable as noting symptoms, none
hitherto penetrating to the root of the trouble. It is only
through accepting the suffering of a genuine but miscon-
ceived advance, through doing the difficult justice at once
to its truth and to its fallacy, that history can find the
argument leading to relief. This argument (which as recognizing a clear dilemma in the very foundations of
modern life is properly called "dialectic") will enable it to
pass out of modernity with its split-mentality into what
lies *beyond modernity*, the era here heralded in whose dawn
we now live.

In this brief work of forecast there can be no attempt to
"cover the ground" of our topic. As befits the temper of
prophecy, I must report only what I am privileged to see.
The connective tissue which makes great books must fall
away. The theme invites a continent: I can offer but a
minor archipelago of say half a dozen islets, with wide
washes of ocean between them. It remains true that what
one thus fragmentarily sees does not announce itself as
"sight" without prior radical analysis. I offer not sporadic
aperçus, but thoughts that chart the forward passage, as
an explorer. Let me therefore name the segments of this
report, having at least a submarine continuity, not Vistas
nor Chapters, but Studies.

The first of these studies will deal with one phase of that
illness of modernity we speak of—a strange powerlessness
that afflicts our majestic institution of public power, the
political state in its proud amplitude and responsibility.
There follows, as a second study, a tracing of the analysis
through which this "Impotence of the State" is understood
and the "Passage beyond Modernity" indicated.

With regard to this second study, the reader may de-
serve a word of comfort. An analysis which finds its way
through fogs of three centuries' standing is not necessarily
easy; but it is also not abstract—on the contrary, it is the
cure of abstraction. Its terminus is, as it must be, an
appeal to the experience of every man. The happy pre-
cision of Berkeley's remark applies to our case: "We have
first raised a dust, and then complain we cannot see!" The
effort we must make is an effort to achieve effortless vision:
whatever is supremely true is supremely natural and
simple. But the effort to achieve effortlessness is not wasted
effort: it adds to the meaning of what is seen; for the

Cartesian period, however rich in fallacy, is at the same time the richest so far in human history in the development of tools for human self-understanding and self-mastery. *The analysis which explains its errors is the analysis which alone secures its fruits.*

This analysis will serve as a usable clue for unraveling the knot of destiny in other phases of the civilization now being born—in particular, the prospects of the greater religions of mankind, their relations to one another and to the emerging common faith.

The welcome arrival of Toynbee's *An Historian's Approach to Religion* as these pages are going to press, hence too late for specific reference here, will lend an historian's dimension of concreteness to the issues with which both are concerned, and an added emphasis to their surpassing gravity and actualness.

In some degree, the two volumes, each in its own way conspectus of a life's work, supplement each other. The present volume might be said to contain a philosopher's approach to history. And quite clearly neither Toynbee nor I suppress the impulse to penetrate veiled regions of futurity. And while we agree that these great issues, involving state, church, secularism, religion, and the possible self-destruction of all civilization, are still in the hands of the gods, we further agree that there are certitudes attainable, and that the event will be shaped by the creative vision and courage of mankind.

WILLIAM ERNEST HOCKING

Madison, N. H.
September, 1956

STUDY I

THE IMPOTENCE OF THE STATE

i. *The State as Developer of Human Nature*

WE RELY on the political community to do its part in the making of men, but first of all to furnish the conditions under which men can make themselves. Through the political community human nature reflects upon itself, discovers the long-run effects of impulsive behavior, learns to curb itself. It gathers the working sense of customs, in which the encounter of impulses has reached adjustments worth conserving. Then comes law, as the coinage of custom consciously criticized, carrying the intrinsic authority—whatever its nominal source—of this agelong interaction of primitive drives. Thus, in positive law, the state sanctions an expression of human nature which human nature has first given to the state.[1]

Prior to and apart from law, the state simply through

---

[1] Here I dwell on the truth that human nature must be an active partner in its own evolving. I do not deny that in a degree the state educates the man, and is "prior to the individual." But I observe that there is no power to educate on the one side, and no right to be educated on the other, apart from the co-operation of the subject. The idea of a "right to an education" as to a commodity transferable from a storehouse to a receiving mind is one of the current symptoms of decay.

1

its continued existence instructs human nature as to its scope. The human will, reasonably or not, concerns itself with posterity, plans for a future beyond its own life span. The presence of the continuing state makes such planning rational: placing at the disposal of its members its own will to endure, the state's time dimension becomes literally theirs. This co-operation of state and person makes possible for each individual a will-to-power-through-ideas, an immortality within human history, in which human ambition may be—we may fairly say—spiritualized.

Thus through the political community man's longer will comes back to him as from an outer source of command. The natural devotion of the human animal to the visible "community of memory and of hope" carries with it a docility to personal discipline such as any whole view imposes on sporadic impulse. The state, purely as secular, comes to be regarded as capable of civilizing the human being, and in so doing of remaking him, training his will, moralizing him.

Human nature has indeed another mirror, and therewith another source of self-training. It has often been the religious community—let us call it in all its forms "the church"—which has promised to give the human individual the most complete view of his destiny and of himself. It projects that destiny beyond the range of human history. It speaks for "the whole"—a totality discernible only by thought—and from a presumed ultimate source of right guidance. It provides standards of self-judgment not alone in terms of behavior, as does the law, but also in terms of motive and principle—of the inner man which the state cannot reach.

In our contemporary world, the secular state tends to

regard itself as the more reliable interpreter of human nature—dealing as it does solely with verifiable experience—and as a sufficient interpreter. It speaks, indeed, not for the cosmos, but for the totality of experience in a community of human beings limited in scope and wisdom; yet still a community whose experience is typical, and may fairly be said to represent mankind. Without pretending to be the universe, it may speak for the universe so far as human science brings it to our ken.

Outside the Marxist orbit, the prevalent disposition of the secular state in recent years has been less to combat the church than to carry on a slow empirical demonstration of the state's full equivalence in picturing the attainable good life, and its superior pertinence to actual issues. As this demonstration gains force the expectation grows that it will be the church, not the state, that will wither away. Where the fields of church and state impinge on each other, as in education and correction, the church will in time appear superfluous. Where they are different, the church will be quietly ignored and dropped as irrelevant.

I do not regard this tacit appeal to the patient pragmatic showing of corporate experience as itself irrelevant. If the state in its secular garb were able to satisfy human nature and succeed in its own work, I should consider that circumstance—not as proof, but as important evidence that the secular hypothesis is valid. And this, not because whatever works is true, but because *whatever is not true will presumably somewhere fail to work,*[2] whether of scientific truth or of truth about the ultimately "real." For whatever is real in the universe is no idle object of speculative fancy; it is a working factor in experience, or it is

[2] *The Meaning of God in Human Experience,* xiii ff., defining a "negative pragmatism."

nothing. Consciously or subconsciously we are always dealing with it: to entertain false ideas about it, or simply to
neglect it, will bring about maladjustments which thrust
the neglect forward into consciousness. Contrary to traditional pragmatism, "experience" is incapable of revising
our ideas for us; it is, however, fully capable of demanding
their revision: a false metaphysic, engendering empirical
malaise, calls for a new work of thought begetting an
altered premiss. This is the "empirical dialectic," [3] a resource of newer modes of thinking. It embodies that
thoughtful respect for a broadened conception of experience which the physical sciences show in their most esoteric
reaches: Einstein himself was to the end seeking a way to
put his final equations to the experimental test. So is every
true thinker about the world. So is the state, as thoughtful
molder of men.

ii. *Two Types of Experiment in Secular Polity*

IN THIS matter of the secular state's premiss, we have at
hand two types of experiment: the explicit experiment of
laïque political constitutions in the present century, expressly rejecting religion as a factor in political life; and
the unintentional experiment of far longer and wider
range—the experiment we call "modernity." For modernity, in begetting a secular science and secular arts, has also
incidentally promoted a secular interpretation of state
and law, even where the *laïque* plunge has not been taken.
   Of this former kind of experiment, most thinking per-

---

[3] *What Man Can Make of Man*, 56 f. The "empirical dialectic" at once
absorbs and corrects the older pragmatism, which assumed that experience could supplant thought and, as it were, make truth true; and
also disposes of the narrow empiricism of sense-data which logical
positivism has recommended to our time.

sons today have had some knowledge. In a generation or two, one with eyes can see a few effects that, within the social maze, can be hypothetically attributed to the experimental omission—in South and Central America, in the United States, in Turkey, in southern and eastern Asia, in the Marxist world. Here, for example, is a Turkish editor with eyes, Ahmet Emin Yalman, writing a series of editorials in his daily *Vatan* in Stamboul during November, 1941, on the topic "Toward Clearness." He notes that "at least in our great cities a whole generation has grown up without any religious influences." This was in some respects "a good thing," for on the older conceptions of religion, "religion could not exist without creating a crisis between the intelligence of a child and his belief." And with a proper education, these religionless young people can become "more dependable, more moral, and more correct." But there are those who "become materialistic. . . . These ridicule the idea of love and of help for others, and consider selfishness and the seeking of self-interest acts of cleverness. They call theft 'free gift' and stealing 'lifting.' They do not believe that one would consequently suffer for one's doings, neither do they believe that tomorrow will bring any good. They want . . . to have every pleasure they possibly can. If these young people could benefit from religion in the ideal sense, they would certainly be better Turks and better human beings. They begin life with a void. . . . We feel very keenly that while other nations in addition to their national unity hold on also to their religious unity, we cannot neglect this binding force for ourselves . . . appropriating the religious factor and giving it a clear place in our social life would be the proper course to follow . . . *every nation needs to build such a bridge between the mind and the feelings.* The Moslem religion is

more suitable for this than other religions." At the head of
this remarkable editorial (Nov. 25, 1941) stands a definition: "The chief role which religion plays is to defeat the
fear and anxiety of today, and to give opportunity for
believing in the good possibilities of the morrow." [4]

My own limited observations lead me to think that these
bolder experiments have had the virtue of most bolder
experiments: they have shown most clearly that with the
clean excision of religion something *politically* essential
has been lost—without any general agreement as to what
that something is. I might venture to formulate a rude
consensus, chiefly negative, to the following effect: that
the secular state by itself is not enough; that just as economics can no longer consider itself a closed science, so
politics can no longer consider itself a closed art—the
state depends for its vitality upon a motivation which it
cannot by itself command.

But it is with the latter experiment, the experiment of
modernity over three or four hundred years, that I am
most concerned. This experiment, which I have called unintentional, as incidental to the outlook creating the ideals
of the secular state, has resulted—if I properly read cause
and effect—in a radical impotence in the very field of the
state's own functions, an impotence only now and slowly
but irresistibly becoming evident, less as from a major
amputation than as from a slight but cumulative malnu-
trition.

Let me point out a number of the less noted symptoms
of faltering in fields in which the state is expected to act,
and has usually acted, with confidence and with a fair

[4] From a translation by J. K. Birge, in "Turkish Translation Service
Letters," ABCFM, Dec. 15, 1941. Italics mine.

degree of success. We have taken it for granted that the state can deal with crime, as its most patent function in sustaining public order. We have believed that it can educate our young. We have assumed that while leaving economic enterprise largely to its own energies, the state can cover the failures of the system, protecting individuals from destitution, caring for the aged and the ill. We have taken it as axiomatic that it can make just laws, and provide through a responsible legal profession for their due service to the people.

We are discovering today, startled and incredulous, that the state by itself can do none of these things.

iii. *The State's Touch on Crime and on Education*

THE state of today is at a loss for a satisfactory—shall we say technique?—in dealing with crime, violent, crooked, or politely corrupt. It has rational codes, well-graded penalties, elaborate and humane institutions: it is building more and larger prisons to accommodate the increasing demand! What better sign of progress? It can apply the penalties. But it cannot punish.

For only the man who has enough good in him to feel the justice of the penalty can be punished: the others can only be hurt, or with a finer realism regard themselves as temporary losers in a game which they may try again. The degree of goodness that alone can give a penalty the quality of punishment is something the state cannot compel. To put it crudely, *only the good man can be punished.* And he would be better without the penalty—he is punished by the judgment.

As for the others, the penalty produces no change of heart. Changes of heart do occur; but it is not the state, and seldom the event, which effects them. And unless they occur, the state faces a dilemma: either it must set the unreformed free into the general community—a confession of futility—or it must imprison them for life, at a cost of human decay, and of moral strain upon the warding personnel, increasingly abhorrent to all who know its nature. If God is dead, the totalitarian answer is correct—mercifully kill the uncompliant. Have we a better answer?

The psychiatrist may suggest abolishing the category of crime, substituting that of disease, and trying a cure. His premiss is false. But he may be allowed to try, and for what palliation he may achieve we are grateful, subject to the comment that he has evaded or postponed the state's issue with the criminal. Nor will the state be easily deluded by the view that abolishing the category of crime has, by the simplest of all methods, disposed of crime itself. Criminology rightly suggests that there are scientific inquiries to be made, and mental conditions to be remedied; but as an art founded solely on such a science, it is bankrupt. Science cannot so much as define the problem of crime; and the state by itself cannot punish.

As with the dealing with crime, so with education, in which broad area the problem of crime is sometimes merged: here is a function the state must perform, and which the self-sufficient state cannot perform. The assumption has been that the modern state can educate not alone the mental person but the volitional person as well. The state by itself can do neither.

As has been noted, the political community both through its laws and through its simple existence always aids in the self-formation of its citizens. The modern state, whether or not avowedly "democratic" always including some degree of popular participation, is peculiarly committed to the belief that education is one of its elementary functions and one of its proudest achievements. This belief tends to become a superstition through disregard of the deep-lying conditions of its partial truth. We are today compelled to note its fallacy.

Consider a mere fraction of the total task, the formal education of children and youth. The state can build schools, equip them; engage a teaching staff; organize and supervise instruction. And in these systems, education usually takes place: it takes place through the personal qualities of teachers who have in them what the state can neither pay for nor command. Vachel Lindsay, the Illinois poet, was a warm proponent of the public school (and so am I); one evening in Beloit, where he had been reading his poetry to high school students, he put the matter to me in this way: "In every primary school of, say, a dozen teachers, there will be one who wakes the children up. And that is enough—for, once wakened, they *stay awake!*" This comment exhibits my point: into the net of the political requirement there happen the genuine spirits who educate. But the political requirement neither produces them, nor tends to select and encourage them. What they do is not literally done by the state.

Especially, in so far as an early cultivation of will and character (a matter in which the home was once the main reliance) devolves upon the schools, can the state provide training for teachers? And can it examine and certify their qualifications? It is like asking whether the state can certify that the teachers have a soul! In a community of normal homes, it has been possible to take a chance on the statistical presence of the unexaminable quality. The chances appear to diminish. But in any case, it is clear

that it is not the state which provides that quality, nor
can it. The state, on its own resources, cannot educate. Let
it magnify without limit its immense volumetric enterprise: its result will still be that of blowing hurricanes
into a cracked flute.

iv. *The State's Touch on Family and on Economy*

I say little of the family. It is the family that stands to
be most immediately sensitive to change in the general
atmosphere of living, such change as humanistic modernity introduced, with its spirit of personal freedom, rightful natural enjoyment, experimental deviation and emancipation from taboo obsessions. These matters profoundly
concern the state; but the state makes no pretense to
inform the family of the life standards of its own institution—it is not directly responsible if there are signs of
disintegration. If there are rising percentages of divorce,
if the "tandem polygamies" of Hollywood provide new
ideals of floating sex association for a self-indulgent community, if parents fail to convince an arriving generation
of the reality of principles they verbally recommend, these
are phenomena whose causes the state cannot reach.

The state can establish legal forms for family life, can
protect its privacy, can ease through law some of its more
tangible strains. But it knows that the life of the home, a
generator of morale for every social activity including
that of the state, must be its own. No power can undertake
to create where creation itself is at home; no power can
mend by law where the spirit of creative love falters. The
patriarchal state employed the family bond for its own
ends; the territorial state, resigning this resource, is helpless to command it. On the contrary, it frequently finds it

serviceable to reverse the dependence, and revive a lan-
guishing *esprit de corps* for itself by invoking the atmosphere of the family—if only by the artifice of the radio
"fireside chat" or by the substantial institution of the
"royal line"—in the relation of government to governed.
Nominally the family is included within the state; morally,
the bond of man to the state is included within, and remains a pensioner upon, the vital bond of man to nature
and all life which is the family. Where there are no
families, there can be no state.

In respect to the economic impulses of labor, acquisition, saving, the state, while far less helpless, is in a similar
situation. Like the basic impulses to family life, so the
economic impulses may be credited to nature; and as
Thomas Aquinas (using the very language of Roman jur-
ists) included the family impulses within the *lex naturae*
as implanted by God and justified by their own existence,
so the modern state tends to assume the economic energies
as given, endlessly self-renewing, and self-justified. The
state may shape and canalize the native dispositions—it
cannot supply them if they are absent.

It cannot, for example, of indolent human clay produce
an industrious society. There are no bitterer chapters in
the history of man's cruelty to man than those burdened
with the effort to compel tropical man into the pattern of
strenuous northern races. Here, race is and remains
tragically important, and equalitarian ideals go blind if
they try to override it, rather than work beneath it.

At the same time, state intrusion is not as in the case of
the domestic impulses a violation; the economic energies
are of tougher substance and admit legal molding. And
while the western states led by England have been dis-

posed for two centuries to a minimum of such molding, and have experimented with an economic near-autonomy, they have discovered that to assume the natural integrity of unleashed economic motives confronts the community with nonpolitical powers that ultimately challenge its own sovereignty. Neither can economic science solve its problems without reference to a wider psychology, an ethic, even a metaphysic; nor can an economic art proceed on the pure maxim that business is business. When the still unsolved problem of distribution appears as an issue of justice, the state can no longer plead nonjurisdiction.

And just at this point, where it must act in behalf of its own standard, accepting responsibility for the spread of well-being in terms of the standard of living, and finding marked success, it becomes aware again of the limit of its ability. It can neither insure that "prosperity" will bring content, nor that labor itself will be, as it normally is, a source of satisfaction. Since the drive for material well-being is capable of expansion without assignable limit, and since the disposition to invidious comparison is constantly whetted by social images of "success," the very advance of economic welfare may become a factor of enlarging discontent. As for labor, the will to give less and less in terms of time and effort for a given real-wage continues—as an artefact of social relations in production—to contaminate the natural joy of the instinct of workmanship. For such self-generated miasmas of motivation the western political community has no medicine. Still less is there cure in that great eastern community professedly of, by, and for labor, in which the most extensive form of punishment is—*labor*; and in which contentedness with one's lot is, in effect, a statutory requirement, enforced by the police. The one spot in all economies in which the natural joy in work is all but inextinguishable, namely, agriculture, is the spot in which the omnipotent state is now having the most radical difficulty, that of maintaining the morale and hence the productivity of the collective farms.

The modern state can neither leave economy to its own play of forces, nor take over its control with success. For economic energies have their norms, their rights and wrongs, partly intrinsic to themselves, partly from general ethics, but partly also from the world view of man and the meaning of his total work, his life's yield; and this meaning the state can neither give nor take away.

v. *The State's Touch on Recreation*

BUT there is another field in which the impotence of the state to control its own moral sources is most strikingly manifest. While easily overlooked as trivial or incidental, it is of vast importance. I refer to the obverse of labor, the occupations of idle hours, the arts of play and the plays of art, the amusements, the prevailing notions of "a good time." [5] Play is the peculiar realm of freedom, and for this reason a fair diagnostic of what the free man fancies his freedom is *for*! What, pray, is freedom for if not for a good time?

Nominally, the function of this freedom is recreation, the unbending of the bow, the renewal of the level of potential energy. But if instead it tends to dissipation, a running down without recharging, it is still our liberty and our pursuit of happiness; and the state is there, is it not, to protect these sacred rights? Who is licensed to

[5] Lecky, in his *History of European Morals,* calls "the extinction of the gladiatorial spectacles" at Rome after A.D. 404 an event "upon which the historian can look with the deepest and most unmingled satisfaction." Vol. II, 40.

instruct us how to enjoy ourselves? Let the state step in to
monitor our good times, or to control the commercial pur-
veyors of our good times, and there is immediate outcry in
the name of the First Amendment, or of some other
charter of liberty.

Shall not the playhouse present what the public will
pay to see? Shall not the publisher be protected in his
freedom to print what the public will buy; his freedom, for
example, to degrade the souls of children through violent,
lurid, smutty "comics"? What are the souls of a few children as compared with his right to make money as his
readers please? If the state draws a line indicating what
is decent to print, and then tries to police the line, it will
in all probability pile up publicity along the border and
make the regulation ridiculous. What experience seems
to show is that both censorship and no-censorship are
failures: stalemate! If there is in the hearts of the people
no revulsion from the degrading of leisure and relaxation,
the state alone—and especially the democratic state—can
do little more than wring its hands, or more probably
shrug its shoulders.

The dilemma is real. *Laissez faire* is acquiescence in slow
disintegration of the texture of social life. Yet law cannot
act without defining its targets, and the integrities of art
and of play elude legal definitions. The effort to explain
and defend dignity lets dignity down. The state is indeed
not without resources other than law. It may enter the
field, as many a municipality has done, with the counter-
attractions of decent play, music, public dance. It may
create recreation grounds, state and national parks and
forest reserves. It may, even in democratic regimes, attempt the traditional role of aristocracy—selective en-
couragement of the nobler arts, as in the Arts Council of

Great Britain. It may, in its basic law, reserve to some authority the power of discretionary and summary action. Great Britain can act "to protect the youth of the country from the influence of certain harmful publications"—as in the Queen's address to Parliament of May 6, 1955—by prohibiting their import, which is a perfect answer, being a mode of the one fit penalty—exile. The degrader should not be killed; he should be put out of the country, or kept out. With like action by all civilized lands, he would discover his due place.

The modern state has forfeited one great advantage of the older political communities—the public force of a sense of honor: "honor" being definable as a respect for the undefinable and unprotectable obligation. And as long as honor has no public power, our civilization is not yet civilized. The state alone cannot civilize.

vi. *The State's Dilemma in Respect to Law*

MY FINAL comment concerns the most intimate and paradoxical field of the state's helplessness, the field of law itself.

The proposition that law is what the sovereign commands is not a nineteenth-century proposal fathered by one John Austin: it is the eternal form of law. All actual law is positive; and all positive law is uncomfortable if it is asserted that the sovereign lawgiver is bound by standards external to himself. Yet it belongs to modernity to make this declaration, and to assert that these standards are to be found not merely in "nature" as *lex naturalis*, but in the human individual as "rights of man." The basis of civil law becomes a pledge of the power of all to secure the rights of each—rights unmodifiable not only by the state but by the subject himself. They are "unalienable." The history of jurisprudence in the nineteenth century is one of continued and varied protest against the legal impossibilities created by this revolutionary conception, the essence of modern freedom.

We are concerned with but one phase of this illuminating struggle, not yet concluded—the inability of any state to administer a code of rights defined as unconditional, and the simultaneous inability of any state to administer the necessary conditions. All legal rights assume an inner lawfulness of disposition on the part of the subject of those rights; let us call it "good will." The presence of this good will is the implied condition of every right— *there are no unconditional rights.* There is no moral right to property, to liberty, to life itself, in the absence of good will. The dilemma of the state is that this condition, as a moral condition, *cannot be legally administered*: there is no legal way to determine its presence or absence. For this reason, the condition is not made a part of the Bills of Rights: it is simply assumed to be present.

And as long as the political morale of the community is in good health, the assumption is satisfactory, with the aid of a few statutory provisions guarding against the more tangible abuses of liberty, as slander, sedition, disorder, et cetera. But unless that public morale is firm, any claim by an individual of "his" rights, as a demand upon the community, is a potential action *against* the community. The loudest right-claimers are today often those who have some private interest to "protect." The spreading menace is becoming apparent; Toynbee has rightly identified it. The usual attitude of western law is that it is better to suffer those abuses of rights which in the run of human nature may be expected, than to limit freedom. The liberty of going wrong is the seamy side of the priceless privilege of going right by free choice rather than by compulsion. But this acceptance of the lesser evil is justified only so long as the volume of abuse is actually minor; and it will be minor while and only while the community at large remains in living touch with its moral sources. A working legal system cannot be had except with the subjective condition: there is no escape.

And since this condition cannot be commanded, the state cannot from its own resources assure the soundness of its system of law, the very center of its *raison d'être*.

vii. *Analysis of the Source of Impotence*

IN NOTING these aspects of deficiency of power on the part of the all-powerful modern state, I am not sounding a litany of defeat. I do not believe in defeat. I look for no *Untergang*, no going under of the western world. A radical analysis of the problem is simply the first requirement for finding a remedy.

In every inadequacy we have noted, the state's incapacity arises from a *failure of the motivation it has hitherto been able to assume in its public.* And since political society is essentially an organization of human wills, *motivation is of its essence.* This bare proposal is all but axiomatic; but the nature of this motivation and the sources of its health are not to be read from the surface of things.

Until recently the psychology of political motivation has been swiftly disposed of by the theorists. In modern political thought, the issue emerged in the guise of a "contract," social or governmental, as expressing the *quid pro quo* offered by Leviathan for the costs of his demands, or as Rousseau's apology for the "chains" of civility and law. In whatever form, these mythical bargains expressed what the writer considered a necessary preference of intelligent mankind for the restraints of the state, in full view of its costs. But a necessary preference can easily sink back into the subconsciousness from which the theorist evoked it. The average man has been innocent of his sagacious bargain, and the modern state has simply assumed "normal human motivation"—in brief, political common sense. The contingency that the habitual obedience which Austin's sovereign could count on might be sapped as by some chronic anemia has not earlier been contemplated, and hence not guarded against.

On the contrary, modernity, favoring the specialization of functions, has tended to encourage the separation of the work of law not alone from morals and religion, but from feeling itself. If Kant is right, the state should exclude motivation from its concern: his central precept of law, *Handle auesserlich so . . .*—"Behave externally so . . .", is in intended contrast with the imperative of morality. Law can require that a debt be paid; but whether from principle, from business prudence, or from a wish to shine, law neither specifies nor inquires. Indeed, few things so embarrass legal procedure as the occasional necessity for inquiring into motive or intention.

Now while Kant is right that the techniques of administering law make it necessary for legal definitions to be framed in terms of behavior, and not of the heart; and while he has won much favor in later jurisprudence for his recognition of this distinction; it is equally clear that he has been misled into an impossible separation. There is nothing on which a free state so much depends as on assent of its people. And as for states that make no boast of

inner freedom, there is still a minimal morale of consent
without which no state can long survive. The police state
is a sick state, on the way to death. Since legal definitions
must be outward, all the more must their implementation
be sustained by the constant gift of *bona fides*: the cynical
query, *quis custodiet ipsos custodes*, may typify the necessarily unguarded gate in every political order where
the issue of life or death for the state is in the hand of an
uncommandable loyalty.

And my thesis is *that modernity has touched western
mankind with some wand that affects this minimal political
morale; and that it is the same wand that has evoked the
miracle of modern liberty.*

For modernity is in principle an alteration in human
self-consciousness; it has received new light as to the
central certitude of the I-think, and therewith as to the
import of the individual human ego. It has accepted the
ethical note corresponding to this certitude, that of the
centrality of the ego that feels, desires, acts. The legal
certitudes of the modern era, inheriting from Roman and
medieval sources the notion of subjective rights, have
framed themselves not on the wide pattern of a common
nature, as with Aquinas, but on the subjective pattern of
the separable ego-substances of Descartes. The "natural
rights" are now perquisites of the individual. *And this
new light is, in the main, a valid light.* Every broad advance in civilization must include a *deepening of subjective sensitivity*, from which source all invention, all the
fertilizing compassions, all art, poetry, prophecy, must be
watered. The spiritual world of modernity, making salient
the moral individual who contains society in himself, and
can stand against all corporate dictation, has a still unex-
hausted invitation to greatness.

This belief is wholly consistent with the judgment that modernity has largely lost the way to ripen the fruit of its genius; and that political life is one of the first sufferers. It is in the nature of the empirical dialectic that it is *the advance that carries the germ of malady*. For a deepening of subjectivity, which enhances sensitivities toward all experiences of good, may at the same time obscure a dimension of every good whatever. I shall now examine this, the crucial point.

STUDY II

PASSAGE BEYOND MODERNITY:

THE POSSIBLE UNIVERSALITY OF SOLITUDE

i. *Modern Subjectivity as Resource and as Threat*

THAT best fruit of modernity, the free individual disposed to stand alone against corporate dictation—what is he standing for? and what is he standing on?

He is standing for his right. But note: he is not standing for his private interest under the specious flag of "my right"; for what he claims as his right he claims *for all others* similarly placed. This is the precise difference between an interest and a right. Further, for the justice of his claim he is prepared to call others—disinterested—to witness. What gives him his footing is the circumstance that this for-others-also situation is at least subconsciously a known situation—known by these others, known also by the corporate being addressed; and that he, the claimant, *knows that it is known.* He seems to "stand alone" —that is his repute; but does he? Examine closely the basis of that strange inner certitude of his: *how does he know* that his situation is known? His aloneness reaches strands far beyond himself. I venture to call the ground

21

on which he stands *a vein of nonsolitude of the "solitary" ego.*

It is the same nonsolitude as that on which Descartes wisely and inconsistently acted when, having lighted on the solitary I-exist as his ultimate certitude—meaning for him I-Descartes-exist—he published it to the world as the basis for all future philosophy! What a load for a private certitude to carry! He instinctively sensed what his method could not justify: namely, that *his private certitude was everyman's certitude in kind.* It had an irrepressible universality. At the extreme depth of his inwardness he joins an infinite outside.

He thus refuted in action the theoretical solipsism derivable from his premises, but without noticing that he had done so. This solipsism has haunted modernity; and modernity has also failed to notice its direct refutation in Descartes' act. Stirred by his enlightening certitude, modernity has followed him gladly into his subjective depths, from which it has drawn wondrous harvests. We have had the monads of Leibniz, the subjective idealisms, *all* the idealisms that draw objects from pure subjects, the inturned romanticisms, and at last the prevailing and all-absorbing psychologisms. All-absorbing, for am not I, the nature-made self, the thinker of all my thoughts? And can any thought of mine escape the coloring of my subjectivity, my pathology, my subconscious drifts and eddies, known only to God, and the psychologist or the psychoanalyst?

Must we not have, therefore, as the perfecting enlightenment, a psychology of all the sciences—a psychology of economics (like Marshall's), of the judicial process (like Cardozo's), of religion (in many versions)—yes, of philosophy also (for has not Jaspers proposed a psychology of philosophical varieties?), even of logic (for are not our pragmatisms, our instrumentalisms and operationalisms, a sort of psychology of thinking?) and hence of physics itself (as in Bridgman's essays)? Should I hesitate to propose a psychology of psychology? Just this was offered to the public, when the Plebs textbooks, issued in London in the twenties, announced in the preface of their text on psychology that it would be a class-conscious production —not guilty of the vice of "objectivity"! Must not our very standards of truth and right—and most obviously, of beauty—be infected with the relativity and warping of the disparate egos, whose problem of togetherness Kant himself never squarely faced?

With this splendid and not infertile depth of inbound separation, the wholeness of man's conscious world is quietly resigned. Alienation from the total-and-real in its unity for all men is aided by the equally wide acceptance of Descartes' complementary doctrine, that physical nature is a process of mathematical perfection which we must conscientiously regard as empty of all purpose and quality: between man and that physical world-total no possible sympathy.

And with this abandonment of man's native rapport with the whole, the nerve of worth in his own living and acting silently ceases to function. Here, I venture to think, is the root of our malady.

For this is the first principle of human motivation: that *meaning descends from the whole to the parts.* The second principle is that meaning ascends from the parts to the whole, the inductive element of value. In every task, the detail sheds its satisfaction or dissatisfaction upward. Driving a nail well is surely an end in itself and sends its items of cheer to the task in hand. But in this continuous

two-way traffic, the significance of the whole has the decid-
ing voice. It can override many an irksome detail, whereas
without it detailed triumphs lose their charm. The worth
of living must indeed have its moment-by-moment verification—total and distant objectives are not enough—but if
one lives determinedly in the present in order to forget
that there *is no ultimate objective*, the nerve is cut.

In childhood, whole-awareness is unquestioned and
latent; it exists as a pervading will-to-live-and-grow-up
in a world credited with wisdom as a firm possession; under
this canopy, the joy of doing is carried by plural pleasure
goals kindly proposed by nature. As we mature, this latent
whole-awareness presents claim as a restless query, *cui
bono*, a demand for total significance, as needed to sustain
the worth of nature's continuing gift. Normally, this demand is met by one's native sense of continuity with the
community, assuming unreflectively—as Descartes did—
the implicit universality of one's private motivation, in the
naïve faith that one's world is a common world, and that
one's private purposes may simply interweave with the
ongoing purposes of that community, and with the dim
world purpose which the unrelenting forward-leaning
spirit of that community foreshadows. Participating in
this thought totality, the meaning of the whole descends
upon the part.

But what if it occurs to me that this is, after all, only
something that "I-think"? What if my naïve faith is precisely contradicted by my philosophy, which assures me
that there is no such thing as a genuine community of
mind? What if this faith is explicitly rejected by the
moving and triumphant science-and-world-view of the
age? Then it is, I say, that the sails of one's will begin to
flop in a failing breeze. The springs of motivation shift

their balance; nature's ostensible pluralism of private
goods tends to resume sway. In particular, that individual
disposed to stand alone for his right reflects that he has
no ground to stand on: for no one can stand on what may
be an insufferable projection of one's private pathology.
The very notion of legal right threatens to yield place to
an attempted calculus of interests.[1]

It is indeed the principle of our advance that has carried the germ of our malady. Deprived of its natural and
responsible objectivity, our individualism begins to show
its capacity to disintegrate, even in youth. And, as an incident, a generation of educators in America seeking a
corrective is thrown into a mad attempt to make education
equivalent to "life adjustment," meaning thereby an artificial collectivizing of the mentality of the young, under
the name of "democracy."

ii. *The Dilemma of Modernity; the Struggle with Solipsism*

OUR situation today is a dilemma. On the one hand, we
cannot repudiate the principle of advance, the subjectivity that has given us the modern individual and his
right. And for this reason we cannot, with Descartes and
unreflective mankind, simply assume the universality of
our private experience. On the other hand, without that
universality, no wholeness and no integration of will.

Because of this dilemma, we cannot end our argument
by proposing simply a return to the religious element in

---

[1] See, for example, Roscoe Pound, *Introduction to Philosophy of Law,*
92–99. Without yielding the field to nineteenth-century social utilitarian-
ism, Dean Pound credits it with "compelling us to give over the ambiguous term 'right.'" His own substitute is derived from the normal
expectancies within a given civilization.

the premodern civilization. We may indeed infer that religion is essential, and this has often been taken as the end of the matter. Religion contains the needed element of union with the whole—this is little more than a truism, for whatever unites the soul of man with the whole is religion.

And herewith we answer at once a question which was early before us: it is clearly *not the destiny of the secular state to render the functions of a religious community superfluous.* On the contrary, with the advance of a technical civilization, a church in our broad sense (assuming that it does its work and nothing but its work) instead of tending to wither away, becomes increasingly necessary to the vitality of the state, its function being to maintain that integrity of motivation which the state requires and cannot of itself elicit or command. This conclusion I regard as valid and important.

But taken as a summons to return to a *status quo ante,* it cannot be sufficient, unless we regard modernity as a false step. If we believe, as I certainly do, that the advances of modernity are genuine, and must enter into the body of whatever faith mankind can hold, we cannot disregard modernity's philosophical quandaries. Philosophy is the good faith of Faith with human thought. The issues raised by philosophy must have an answer for reason as well as for intuition. Faith itself will be affected by what we here require—a new advance of thought which, without losing the modern depth of subjectivity, can give us a rational right to our "naïve assumption" of the universality of our private experience.

In the search for a releasing insight, modernity has been held fast by its own postulates—among them this, that what is subjective cannot at the same time be shared: there is no such thing as a literal awareness by one mind of another mind. The other's selfhood can certainly not be sensed, nor can another's experience be experienced as he experiences it. The first person plural, "we," is half hypothesis. When you and I look at "the same object," all I surely know is that I look at it, and suppose there is a "you" who does the same. In brief, there is no genuine consubjectivity (or as it is commonly referred to, no "intersubjectivity") for a scrupulous modern empiricism: the word "we" is a trap for the unwary!

Hence when my colleague Whitehead, in one of our joint seminars, throws out in an amiable aside, "Hang it all! *Here we are*: we don't go behind that, we begin with it," he has implicitly brushed aside one of the theoretical bases of modernity. He speaks the common sense of mankind; and in my judgment he is entirely right. But to justify the stroke, we must explicitly alter the bases of our epistemology.[2]

In practice, each individual mind, having its unique perspective of a world, includes therein its fellow minds: each *believes* in the existence of his fellows. There are no solipsists-by-belief. Yet, on Descartes' ground, which is modernity's, we must all, with Leibniz and Bertrand Russell, be *solipsists-in-theory*. As Kant has perfectly put the matter, "The I-think must be able to accompany (and swallow) all my *Vorstellungen*"—all my ideas and perceivings. On this point, Leibniz alone is fully consistent (and more resolutely consequent than Kant, who evaded the issue of the "we"): minds are monads, each with an impenetrably private world panorama unrolling, not before him, but in him.

---

[2] I have discussed this point at length in "Marcel and the Ground Issues of Metaphysics," *Philosophy and Phenomenological Research*, June, 1954, 447 ff.

Could there be such a thing as a veritable consubjectivity whereby one self participates, not by imaginative or
sympathetic construction, but by actual experience, in the
selfhood of another? Could this be the case without de-
stroying the privacy of the ego, so that our physical
world, for example, could be literally a common world, and
known as such, without any intrusion of person on person?
If that were the case, we should see and judge things with
a natural universality. The solitary experimenter would
know (as he spontaneously assumes) that his results must
be confirmed by everyone who follows the experiment
under the same conditions: a universal science would be
justified. Each man would be, not merely an I-think, but
man-thinking. This, I submit, seems to be not only the true
state of affairs, but the necessary state. And if our philosophy fails to allow it, perhaps we must change our
philosophy!

Such a paradoxical immediacy of otherness—at once a
true realism (for our "phenomena" would thus acquire the
immediate objectivity they seem to have) and a true idealism—would constitute the dilemma-solving insight. Modernity, through the firm logic of its subjective certitude
and the derived empiricism of private sense data, must
reject it as impossible. It becomes necessary in our philosophy to *pass beyond modernity.*

iii. *Political Theory Makes an Effort:*
Partial Solution

LET us note in passing that contemporary political
theory shows signs of recognizing this quandary and of
moving toward a solution.

It has well outgrown the stage at which the subject's obedience has to be understood as a contract or counsel of prudence. It listens with less than half an ear to the present school of "legal realists" disposed to interpret law as a "threat," as if most of us were at heart transgressors. Without too heavy an investment in the nonrational impulses proposed by the various depth psychologies, it recognizes that rationalistic egoisms are not plausible descriptions of human nature. Primitive impulses, such as the herd instinct, and the natural dispositions of the human will to serve, through family, clan, posterity in general, aims outreaching private good, insufficient as they are for a developed theory, at least point the way to a more adequate psychology of political life.

With a realer realism, political theory now perceives that the will to obey has permanent sources in what men think and believe about their total environment—in cosmic bearings and allegiances not supplied by the visible community. With great courage, Professor Robert MacIver points out that the "web of government" is sustained in part by an element of "myth." Why myth?

Myth seems on the face of it a step into the vague— something less tangible or structurally useful than those ideal standards—truth, justice, beauty, et cetera—which ancient philosophy singled out as universal guides for the human will. These guides the Stoic legalists could specify for legal use and Justinian's codifiers hand on to the lawmakers of Europe. Modernity, however, has dealt hardly with these standards; it is bound on its own principle of subjectivity to reduce all principles (including its own) to the level of psychological variables. Are they not creatures of the subjective I-think? I look on them with a sentiment of regard; but have they a footing in the nature of things

beyond my psychological setup? Here myth may inject a
word.

What myth adds is the suggestion—through song and
story, through its appealing store of admirabilia and
detestabilia—that they *may have* such a footing. The quiet
molding of wills through the pictured decisions and characters of gods and heroes is empirically near-universal.
Religion goes farther: it adds the responsible assertion
that they *do have* such a footing—as world view, *religion
is the affirmation of the anchorage in reality of ideal ends.*
Myth, as the more tentative position, may well be more
agreeable to the scientific temper: it is confessed hypothesis, whereas religion is dogma. But it contains the important advance, an escape from psychological debility to
the outer air of speculative metaphysics—the word "speculative" here meaning "inquiring"!

This escape is essential. But it must be justified. The
dilemma of modern thought has been created by philosophy, and philosophy, not imagination alone, must re-
solve it. How can we keep the treasure of subjective depth,
and at the same time retain hold on universal validity in
our experience?

iv. *Passing beyond Modernity: Intersubjectivity and Participation*

It is the present century that has met the persistent
philosophical issue.

The revolt against subjectivism had begun earlier. A
sturdily growing social science could not operate with
closed individual selfhoods. The quandary of solipsism had

to be overcome or broken through. There was an inviting
path much followed prior to the turn of the century—that
of resolutely dissolving the supposedly impenetrable ego
in the social milieu, showing how far the development of
the I-think is molded by language and social interaction.
There was important truth along this path (as followed by
Mead, Baldwin, and others) ; only, Descartes' logic was
not thereby met, it was submerged in the advancing wave
of psychological sociability. And if this were the whole
truth, the prize of modernity's deepened subjectivity is
surrendered—the proud and pregnant loneliness of free
individual creativity and right.

The solution was achieved by an opposite path—one
which in the end made full use of the new social insights,
but which began by following further the logic through
which the quandary appeared, aided by a more perceptive
analysis of what we call "experience."

"Experience" is modernity's magic word of charm.
"Experience" is the suggested sum, or integral, of all the
items, the dx's, of human empiricism. The word is con-
veniently noncommittal as to *whose* experience is implied
—whether my sole-own, or ours—yours-and-mine, or perhaps mankind's-in-general. It suggests, without asserting,
an actual world-wide consubjectivity (as we have above
termed the genuine "we," p. 27) such as would exist if
the ego and its fellows shared an identical object. What
the newer analysis has discerned *within "experience"*—
and what Plato and Descartes and Kant had failed to find
there—is *an intersubjective Thou-art*, inseparable from
each subjective I-am, serving to bind their several experiences together in such wise that the loose suggestion of a
shared experience with an identical object is defined and

confirmed. The idea of a literal consubjectivity toward a common world object is realized.

For note: As the term "experience" is noncommittal as to the identity of the subject or subjects who are experiencing, so the term "I-think" is equally noncommittal as to the experience or experiences it includes. Descartes left the matter open: he failed to mention the *content* of the I-think as essential to its existence, and accordingly passed no judgment as to whether this content need be *exclusive* in order that the I-think hold its identity. Now the only condition under which any self can be aware of its own existence is that it is occupied with some content; and clearly the sole possibility that any self should enter the experience of another is that *some content*, some bit of experience, should be not exclusive but *had in common*, and known to be common. If experience could thus be shared, directly or through some third subject, solipsism is at an end, and yet without the fusion of self into self.

What we can now verify is that private experiencing, as receptive, is a certain *participation* of each I-think in the experience of an intersubjective Thou-art. Through this participation, my experience acquires the substantial "objectivity" of being no private dream of my own. And so far as these participations extend to all, our common objects enter the single *world unity* common intuition has always assumed them to have.

But further, the presence of this uniting selfhood provides the assurance that the common experience of mankind has an indwelling purpose, a *telos*, in which the I-am also participates. My aims cease to be mere psychological distillates of private passions; they have "an anchorage in reality." Therewith a way of hope opens for the individual, groping for significance.

v. *General Course of the Philosophical Argument*

To SKETCH briefly the path by which this result has been reached:

Solipsism, we have noted, has never been believed; but it has frequently been taken as an inescapable incident of our being *selves,* each with an unsharable center of feeling and perspective reference, whose intimate continuities of experience-and-memory-and-wish are only fragmentarily communicable in the coin of common speech. The logic of solipsism has been taken most seriously by the most strenuously logical thinkers, as by the early Bertrand Russell following Leibniz, and by the later Edmund Husserl. This was the necessary course of philosophical honor, if the "egocentric predicament"—to use Ralph Perry's perfect phrase—were to be logically overcome and not simply broken through in favor of the claims of common intuition.

The first step in this logical overcoming was the recognition that the solipsist position contains a self-refutation. It is not merely inconsistent with our natural behavior, as when solipsists commune with their fellows, or when Mrs. Ladd-Franklin, solipsist by logical conviction, writes to Bertrand Russell expressing "surprise that there are not more of us." It is further inconsistent with its own assumptions. For the proposition "I am incurably alone" implies that I know what being-alone is contrasted with: the proposition is significant only if I know what it would be to be not-alone. But if I were constitutionally alone I would be unaware of that fact, having no conception of the opposing condition of being. Leibniz must get mentally out of his monadic window and circulate among the monads in order to know that none of them, including his own, has windows! In brief, no one can speak or think universally of the monads unless monadism is a fallacy. To take Descartes literally is thus, in the end, to break with Descartes.

But shall the break be a simple repudiation, or shall it be by way of a more incisive logic?

For the most part, philosophy at the turn of the century acted by repudiation, and the substitution of alternative theories of knowledge. Henri Bergson reinstated "intuition" (1903) as a cognitive resource, able to "coincide" with its objects, including other selves and the semipurposive *élan vital*. This cures solipsism in a convincing way, since Bergson's intuition is every man's intuition made systematic and responsible, and the cure is valid. But since it acts by *force majeure*, i.e., by simply endowing one cognitive function with the power of self-transcendence (as the older dogmatic realisms did for all cognitive functions), the intellectual problem remains unsolved; and Bergson, by disqualifying the "intellect" in metaphysics, waived the effort to solve it.[3]

[3] The resurgent realisms of this period followed in the main the path of repudiation, asserting a natural power of self-transcendence in human knowledge, and rejecting extant attempts to express the "objectivity" of the natural world as a domain of thought or (with Royce) of purpose. Royce and others in America and Simmel in Berlin felt more definitely responsible for the underlying problem, how any awareness of a mind-not-one's-own is possible. The answers tended, as in the metaphysic of Kant, to shift from the rational to the moral: the other mind is a being we *ought to acknowledge*, not aspire to experience. Whitehead was later to offer the most radical repudiation of solipsism, by quietly discarding the entire causal account of perception (of which subjectivism is an inescapable corollary), in favor of a theory of "prehensions" involving direct other-awareness.

Meantime Husserl, in Göttingen, with the utmost logical care and scruple, had opened his campaign against one aspect of subjectivism, *Psychologismus*, making salient the "intentional" factors of thinking, and invoking *"Wesensschau,"* a perceiving of concepts, to guarantee their validity. This analysis remained interior to the Cartesian I-think; it was, as he later called it, "egological." It was not until his Parisian Lectures of 1929 that he explicitly faced the issue of solipsism, and reached a

The second and affirmative step in the overcoming of solipsism remained to be taken. It depended on a consideration closely following the first step; namely, that since we do have the conception of aloneness, it must also be true that we have the conception of not-aloneness; and that conception we could not get by solitary imagination —the materials of a solitary experience do not provide the right kind of otherness to construct the idea of other-mind. The conception of companionship is possible only if there is somewhere the actual experience thereof. *Solipsism is overcome, and only overcome when I can point out the actual experience* which gives me the basis of my conception of companionship. There must be such an experience of other-mind-present, not reducible to an I-think-enjoying-a-pantomime-companionship. The problem is to identify this experience beyond possible recapture by my all-embracing subjectivity.

The quest has its difficulties. Minds are not perceivable as are the bodies to which we attribute mentality. Our voluminous and skillful intercourse with our fellows is developed on the basis of an immensely successful hypothesis that such-and-such visible and tangible objects are *signs* of mentality-and-purpose: the hypothesis of signs implies a prior idea of other-mind-expressing-itself-by-signs. What we are interested in is *the origin of that prior idea*—an idea for which there could be no corresponding sensation. It must be present very early, for infants appear to use it; and if truly intersubjective, then pervasive, and like all continuous experiences almost evanescent. We must be prepared to think that it has no determinate

---

position which he described (with a precise ambiguity) as "monadological intersubjectivity" (*Husserliana*, I, 121 *et passim*, 1950). Solution incomplete.

beginning; that each one is always consciously participating in the life of an Other, inseparable from his own sense of being, even on the preconceptual level of bodily awareness. How can such an experience be traced or identified?

We are helped by recalling, what we have already observed, that Descartes, in singling out the I-think as the fulcrum of his lever, has left us with an unfinished expression. There is no I-think (period). It is always I-think (something). An empty mind is not even idly contemplative: the vacant mind is simply nonexistent. If the premiss is *cogito nihil*, the inference has to be *ergo non sum*—an inference which the ego would be in no position to draw!

I do not mean to say that Descartes' omission of the something-thought-about was an oversight. Finding that he could doubt the existence of whatever object, and as his *chef d'oeuvre* of doubt that of the world itself, he felt free to concentrate his certitude of existence on the thinking process. Not dismissing stuff-thought-about, he was simply suspending the attribution of existence to that stuff, precisely as Husserl has done in his *epoché*. But if it is granted that my empirical existence depends on a continuous I-think-something-empirical (presumably with a rill of sense data at the base of it), I can only be sure I exist if something (else) exists also. In order to be valid the Cartesian certitude requires to be enlarged: *cogito aliquid ergo sum, et aliquid est:* I think something, therefore I exist, and something (else) exists. It still remains true that my thinking involves my existence; the point is, it involves more.

Indeed, the proposition that I can doubt the existence of every object of thought is a fallacy. For to doubt existence is to know what it is that I doubt—I must know what I mean by the existence of the object. And I can know this

only if there is a knowable difference between the existent
and the nonexistent object, in which case it would be impossible to doubt the existence of objects presenting the
known criterion. The doubt is thus either meaningless or
self-defeating.

We arrive at the position—not without a suggestion of
paradox—that something of the not-self is essential to the
existence of the self. The matter becomes clear when we
consider what we mean by sense data. Data are things
given; and what is being "given" is in transit from an
outer source to a receiver—only in this case what is given
is not a detachable commodity, it is an essential factor in
the being of the receiver. That is what "experiencing"
literally is—a process in which the not-self is continuously
becoming self. In the incessant rill of the empirical strand
of living, always including sensation, the self is being
sustained in being. To that extent we may say it is *being
created*.[4]

We might now take it as a self-evident proposition that
whatever creates a self can only be a self. We should then
have arrived at our goal. Our empirical receptiveness to
the sensed world is something more crucial and inward
than an observing of variegated qualities out-there: it is
also a receiving of my own life from a life-giving entity,

---

[4] "However vigorous the impetus of advance-weaving on the part of
my ideas (my active expectations of experience just ahead) . . . my
own activity always accepts the irruptive (sense-) material as its own
authority and completion. Toward that outer reality I hold myself as
toward that which sustains me from moment to moment in my present
being. Is not that outer activity then essentially creative . . . creative
of *me?" The Meaning of God in Human Experience*, 286 f.

We may recall in this connection a speculation of Descartes to the effect
that God does not create once and then leave his world to itself, but that
he re-creates the world from moment to moment. In a similar sense, the
constancy of the empirical contribution to the mental being of the
receiver is a reiterated creation.

which can by no stretch of imagination be a physical "stimulus" and nothing more. It is not a causing; it is a communicating; it is the primitive Thou-experience. The causal account of perception, valid and necessary as accounting for relationships among sense data, ceases to be remotely plausible as the essence of the transaction.[5]

vi. *Appeal to Immediate Experience*

But dispensing with further argument, let me now rather seek to evoke in the reader that awareness which must be the final evidence of our result. For what we are here asserting is an element in the experience of every person: it must be verifiable there.

We do not ordinarily consider the world we perceive as an activity upon ourselves. We perceive it as a *simple thereness* of the sense-presented expanse. And there is no I-think in the picture. We can go all the way with Hume, who discovers no "self" among his impressions: by no possibility can the self be a sense object. To catch a glimpse of one's self requires a shift of vision, a turn which we call "reflexion." One can always make this turn, and always find the I-think on duty; especially when I am in doubt as to what I see, or am challenged. "I saw an airplane." You doubt it? "*I think* I saw one"; I retreat to the asylum of certitude. Or "What is this I see? I think it's a

[5] The causal theory of perception terminates strictly speaking in brain processes, not in percepts. These brain events, if they could present worlds at all, would present as many private worlds as there are private brains. The terminus of the theory is thus inconsistent with its starting point in the common physical world, even if we forget the now widely recognized necessity of assuming a miracle to translate brain event into perception; and this scandal remains unremoved. The theory, useful for relationships, is bankrupt as an account of perception.

far-off plane—it may be a bird"; I ask your corroboration.

The same turn that brings the I-think into the picture brings also the sharableness: the simple thereness is already *common* experience, common receptivity toward an intersubjective action. Yet as action it is wholly different from any activity I might perceive in the field of thereness: it is silent, unrelenting, with no insistence on change, more like a firm pressure-of-being from the unnamed, unvocal, nonintrusive Other. I recognize it as the will of another self, a purposive selfhood, purposing among other things the being of this I-think. It is the Thou-art, immediately experienced as such.

Even so, the Thou-art is not salient. In its aboriginal form, it is a constant vital fact, beneath the level of concepts: it may be intrauterine as a vague awareness of dependent being, with an equally vague possibility of address-of-discomfort to the surrounding universe. But there is a point at which this locus-of-address becomes distinct and recognizable:

"Experiencing," as a rule, while we receive what is given, is also an activity on our own part—an activity of attention, more or less awake and alert. This activity is so far spontaneous that we do not associate it with a sense of effort. There arises, however, in the course of conscious development, an issue of free effort in dealing with what is given. Sense data by themselves constitute no "world." There are two ways of taking them. We may steep ourselves in their immediate quality for the purely aesthetic enjoyment of that quality—the incipient epicure or artist in all human nature. Or we may, with an effort of thought, work them into patterns of "object" and "event" which move toward responsible living, in the end to science itself. Descartes in his view of the I-think raises no issue of this effort—his broad expression includes the whole range of sensing, feeling, willing, et cetera, as well as the intentional "thinking" involved in forming a coherent world picture. What, I now ask, is your incentive for this effort to think a world?

It is—and here I venture like Descartes, but with better justification, to interpret your experience for you—it is something like *an intimation of your destined way of living.*

The world I *think*, as distinct from the nonworld I *sense*, is a range of experience sharable with others. If I am to live as my *élan vital* spurs me to live, I must live in a field of experience not mine alone. But my first note-of-call is not from these many unidentified fellows: it is from the inner source of the sense-presented expanse, with which source I am aware of a certain kinship. My impulse to live by thinking, rather than by sensing alone, is a *response* to a felt purposiveness of the real with which in experience I have to do. It is akin to that sense of duty, which to Kant was our most direct approach to being-in-itself. But it is a wider thing. It is the apprehension of a way of life that Life assigns me; it is a sort of compass needle toward self-fulfillment and duty at once, in one urge of will direction. If there is in it a sense of the right of the universe against me, commonly called "duty," there is equally a sense of my right as against the universe that has thrust life upon me: if there is any obligation at all, it is reciprocal. And both senses imply the prior awareness that the source of things is a Thou—a Being fit on the one hand to receive my note of protest where protest is due, and on the other hand to pervade my living with a sense of expected performance.

For Kant, the primary and inescapable reality of duty is the source of our postulate of God. In this order of things, the actualities of experience are reversed. Unless there is first a known being to whom duty can be due, there *can be no duty*. And there is more than duty, more than reciprocal duty, in the actual situation. There is, as I shall later emphasize, an element of faith-in-opportunity; a hopeful launching out on the effort to achieve the costly happiness of becoming what I am destined to become. All this is wrapped up in the spontaneous impulsive summoning of one's will-to-think, the simplest and most general *response* to the presence in experience of the universal Other-mind.

The strength and persistence of that response is seen in the corporate and historic edifice we call "science," a building surely not made with hands. This building testifies to the assurance whereby our monadic worlds are known as one world; and whereby the lonely experimenter, wherever he is, knows his discovered truth as unquestionably a truth for every man.

With this assurance, verified in experience because arising there, we have passed beyond modernity into the post-modern era.

vii. *Juncture of Philosophy and Religion at a Deeper Level*

I HAVE presented this result as the outcome of an experiment, the "unintentional experiment" of modernity. It is at the same time a dialectical result; for any experience of commitment to a thought must be a thought-filled experience. It is through *carrying the logic of solipsism to the end* that its cure is found. Modernity has thus held to its own type of certitude, its science, its humanistic confidence in human thinking—in brief to its "I-think"—until on its own empirical ground it sees its incomplete truth.

What religion may say, and truly say, is that this intersubjective reality is nothing other than its own eternal and unswerving doctrine of God, whose meaning in human experience is now belatedly discerned. To which Modernity might be conceived to reply, "That is true; and religion's honor also is to hold to its own certitude. But that certitude has not hitherto been held, nor could it be held, as an answer to the question which I, Modernity, alone have raised. It is I who have descended deepest into the Hell of the soul's solitude. And having through the agony of my own loyalty to truth at last been able to say, 'Behold Thou art there,' I add for all future time that dimension to the meaning of religion."

Herewith the question inevitably emerges whether the reconceived religion which thus takes form as an answer to the dilemma of modernity is to be the Christian religion, or some other of the great religions, or some development beyond them.

But first, an interlude on how civilizations rise and fall —and how far!

STUDY III

THE STRUCTURE OF HISTORY

i. *Résumé: Tentative Outlook for State and Church*

OUR concern is with the shape of the civilization to come. As guiding lines we consider especially the place in that civilization of the state and the religious community, since each of these undertakes in its own way to reflect and satisfy the whole of human nature.

We have first examined the state. For if, as intelligent humanists, we can get on without religion, the state becomes our trust. However great our faith in the human individual, we have never thought him self-sufficient. Man is a creator; but he is a creator who must first be created. If it were only on the basis of everyday wants, he must live in society; and while the economic necessity is instructive as to his shaping and being shaped, we are today less than ever persuaded by the Marx-Engels following—illuminating for its time—that the logic of his economic needs can explain man's social history or his cultural prowess, still less outline his destiny. As modern men, we still see with Aristotle the political community as the specific instrument of "the good life" in its human amplitude; and modern man still nearer approaches Aristotle's persuasion

43

that in this respect the state is "nearly if not quite self-sufficient." [1] We recall that Greece had almost nothing corresponding to a church. As for economy, we see that it is the political community that shapes the economy, not the economy that makes the nation.[2] It is the state which holds within the grasp of a unified will-to-power both the economic and the social needs of man.[3]

This does not mean that we have ever mistaken the state for the cosmos, or imagined that for practical purposes the state is equivalent to "the whole." We simply see in it the one representative of the totality of being *with which we can converse*: it is for us the responsible, and in general the responsive, image of the whole of things. We may in a sense pray to it, and sometimes be heard: of what other symbol of totality can this be said? The state, like all things human, is finite: and the gap between the finite and the infinite remains—infinite. If, as some say, and I am with them, it is with the infinite that we have always to do, the state must be infinitely short of complete competence. Agreed. But the gap that is logically infinite may be psychologically negligible. If, as seems evident, everything tangible is finite, and the state's purview reaches to all the relevant tangibles, trust in the state, slowly perfectible through infinite time, seems the path of available wisdom. Secular modernity has, in effect, committed itself to this experiment. We have followed some of its findings.

At this its strongest point, we have found modernity vulnerable, and with modernity, the state. Its Achilles' heel, if we are right, is not itself a tangible and overt weakness—say the rationalizing or technicalizing of society, or

---

[1] *Politics*, 1252 b.
[2] *Man and the State*, 296.
[3] *Ibid.*, 330.

the functional character that thus descends on the individual's self-definition, or the simple existence of the "mass man" with his diminished and derivative mentality. These are indeed disturbing traits of the life of modern man, proud in his newly won dignity, freedom, and scientific power, and those who, like Ortega y Gasset, dwell on them are on the right scent. But as evils-flowing-from-goods they are, I believe, symptoms of a malady simpler and deeper rooted, an inner surrender, the gradual abandonment of the individual's native rapport with a genuine—not representative—total-and-real, an immediate Thou-art, which is at the same time his avenue of rapport with his fellow men.

With this surrender has come the tacit relinquishment of his certitude of the universality of his private experience and therefore of his confidence. For man in the same moment, and by the same fact, that makes him solidary-at-root with his tribe and with humanity, is individualized and set beyond crowd pressures. It is his private tryst with the Absolute, whereby his certitude is at once every man's certitude so that he can think and speak for man-in-general, that normally enables him to hold his own in presence of whatever strains arise from social organization. Losing that rapport, he loses what makes him a state-sustaining being. The state by itself cannot insure its own perpetuity.

This diagnosis, which I have offered as an experimental and also as a dialectical outcome of modernity, exemplifies an ancient paradox, the paradox of power. The secular state has become not only the greatest of tangible powers, but in concrete terms, the sole power—the trusted repository of all the physical forces of the community. And Leviathan at the peak of his all-might is lamed. By what?

By deficiency in the field of motivation, a lack of control in the region of "mere feeling." It is the nonassertive Tao of Lao Tze that still bends the strongest to its demand.

But while a diagnosis may and should point to a remedy, it is not itself a prescription. The integrating of human motives is the business of religion; but religion is not a commodity that can be prescribed, nor is it a staple. It exists for itself alone, and while always the same, as the bond between the soul of man and the Real, it varies internally with its specific tasks. For what that bond requires depends on the depth and character of the separation between the soul and its object due to varying experience and thought. The Real is by definition eternal; but the religious questioning of modern man is not necessarily met by the expositions of religion for premodern man. That issue lies before us.

Meanwhile, if we may tentatively assume that there exists a mode of religion prepared or preparable to mend the lost rapport between the modern soul and the Absolute, our analysis provides certain indications of the role of its community in any future civilization.

Because religion can never serve as a "means only"—a means for curing the ills of the state—the dependence between church and state is not mutual. *The state is dependent for its vital motivation upon an independent religious community.* It must therefore allow the free exercise of religion so far as religion is honest—i.e., so far as it serves its function of integrating the human will in view of the whole—simply because nothing that is not free and universal can be religion.

This duty of the state does not infringe the state's conceptual sovereignty, nor is it in general onerous. It leaves sovereignty intact, because the duty in question is not a legal duty: it is a duty arising simply from the logic of the state's self-preservation.

It is not, in general, onerous, because the civilized state takes it for granted that its citizens are full-grown men, having their own hold on principle; it knows that it can be served only by individuals who are first of all servants of truth and honor. To this extent, the modern state is entirely at home with the principle that the primary loyalty of its subjects is and ought to be beyond itself. At the same time, the possibility of clash between state and church is written into the situation.

For example, the religious community is by definition universal in extent as well as in norms of will: it speaks not primarily to the man-within-the-nation but to the man-within-the-world. It spins the web of a potential world society. Reaching across all boundaries it fosters a moral unity among men without which international order lacks a necessary precondition—that of psychological fraternity. For peace and order must be built on mutuality of feeling before they can be built on laws and powers. This preliminary work toward world community can never be of indifference to the state. On the whole it tends to be in accord with national purposes; but it can bring a radical criticism to bear on national egoism, the more effective as its own fellowship becomes actually as well as intentionally world-wide.

And the state has no choice but to accept this possibility of clash, whether in foreign policy or in domestic affairs, a possibility which—in spite of all efforts to make a firm line between the standards of politics and morals—effectively limits its freedom of action to courses that do not massively violate the consciences of its people. The state has no choice, because the subjects for their part—unable to escape their knowledge of the state's finitude—have themselves no choice but to find their primary loyalties in whatever glint they may discover through inward clues of an absolute good.

It can never be the state's duty—as premodernity sometimes assumed possible—to deduce positive law and policy from the premisses of religion and ethics, for which these premisses are incompetent, as Aquinas clearly saw. But it will always be the duty of the state, unless by persuasion it can transvalue the values of its people, to create policies that do not contradict these premisses. This is a principle of politics as old as Confucius, in which Machiavelli shrewdly concurs, a principle which will remain valid as long as the state must live in the freely accorded respect and consent of its members.

But if the state has a duty, so has the church. For the continuing historical community of religion, undertaking to offer an unshakable world affirmation in which primary loyalties may be anchored, must probe the depth of the soul's lostness in the given era of man's thought, even while distraction and despair may be far off. Religion has frequently to disturb the undisturbed, to create anew a sense of that moral aloneness-with-the-Absolute which is the sole security against the anaesthesia of crowd insouciance. For the individual, circumstance and the current temper may benumb his "cosmic anxiety"; yet that anxiety remains a measure of his realism, not of his folly, it must be the groundwork of all his building. Religion must always spur the soul not to evade experience nor new-opening truth but to descend into the caverns, psychological and other, that science or public crisis may open for exploration. Religion must *descend with the soul*, while keeping intact the thread of recovery of a true universality. "Saving the soul" in this sense must be the ever-renewed and ever-changing duty of religion.

It becomes here especially apparent that in this duty the state has no competence; and yet depends for its vitality on that well-grounded firmness of character which it cannot of itself supply. With this understanding, the relation of church and state cannot be either now or in the future one of rivalry, nor of duplication in the task of interpreting human nature. It is a natural symbiosis, on the ground of the priority and autonomy of the religious consciousness.

ii. *Obliteration of Historic Rhythm: the Unlosable*

BUT what can we discern of the shape of the civilization that is to succeed what we call modernity? What guidance can history give us as to the passage toward recovery? Is humanity perhaps following a rhythm, now passing from its upward to its downward phase, so that we must anticipate a period of confusion, if not of *Untergang*?

History has indeed its repetitions of rhythmic tracery, lending force to the judgment that civilizations, too, are mortal. But as a whole, history never repeats; partly because civilizations have seldom perished—perhaps never *in toto*. Commonly in their phase of ebb they have injected something of their essence into a rising movement elsewhere, ruder and fuller of will-to-live—within chaos, continuity. By whatever it thus inherits, that rising movement starts from an altered level, excluding the concept of recurrence. Is this inherited element ephemeral and accidental, or may some of it keep its place?

There is in history a certain tough cumulativeness at

two levels—levels at which mankind cannot forget—the level of technic and the level of insight. At these levels there is set into human nature *a mental ratchet* which prevents total slipping back, a selective holding function which can easily escape notice amid apparently unlimited change. Arts have been lost, but not all arts—the art of fire-making, the taming of animals, the conquest of the sea, the art of printing. . . . Sciences have been lost, even astronomies and geometries, but not the multiplication table, nor once devised in India the arithmetical zero, nor once mastered in Greece the science of proof. . . . Poetry is born profuse as the flowers of the field, and vanishes as they do; and there is poetry the race cannot forget. . . . Religions likewise. In religion, the unforgettable may be more evident than the rationally final, and perhaps ought to be.

I point out simply that there are odd durabilities that cut through the vast rhythm of rising and falling civilizations, checking each fall at a higher point, and that may in due time put an end to the ending. History, for good reasons, finds it hard to identify the cumulative characters. Yet unless they are recognized the total structure of history threatens to be that of a record—on the one hand of perpetual passing, *das Einmalige*, or on the other, of the recurrent and sterile, losing sight of its most significant ingredient, *the unlosable*.

If through the role of the unlosable—without appeal to any "law of progress"—we can eliminate to some extent the rule of rhythm, and so of periodic downfall in the broad swing of human affairs, as well as of the "eternal recurrence," might we not with the same stroke *eliminate the element of plurality* in our picture of civilization? In my judgment, this is now taking place.

iii. *Elimination of Plurality of Civilizations*

TODAY, we seem to stand on the threshhold of a new thing, civilization in the singular. We still have civilizations: the distinction between The East and The West still has validity. And what Toynbee calls the aggression of the West upon the East has had an indubitable basis in fact. But whether it has been the whole fact, I doubt; and certainly, it has long ceased to be the main part of the fact. Much of what was once transmitted from West to East by the methods of imperialism has become self-propagating —first imposed, then sought, then demanded as of right. A siphon flow has usually to be forced to begin with. No one who has seen a western technical school in the Orient, or an agricultural station, or a hospital, can entertain the picture of "aggression" as the dominant fact in these fields, though aggression has frequently been the frame in which these transactions have occurred.

In any case, our present period is one of general and reciprocal osmosis of thought, technique, art, and law. The assimilation proceeds from both sides; though the West is only beginning to realize its potential property in the unlosables of the East. These processes can neither be stopped nor undone; the lines that have "gone forth into all the world" cannot return to their origin. The making of a single civilization is contained in the two concepts, the universal and the unlosable, plus the simple existence of the arts of unlimited human communication.

Hence we may say that for the first time our entire world space is permeated with ideas which, as Locke said about truth and the keeping of faith, "belong to man as man and not as a member of society." Here and there in the Orient there is still revulsion from clinging localisms of western thought and practice, but none toward what we may call the Clean Universals, the sciences, the mathematics, the technics—these it claims *not as borrowings from the West, but as its own.* In giving birth to the universal, the West has begotten something that can never again be private property.

For the first time, too, among these ideas are certain discoveries of the inner dynamics of material particles which deliver into our hands the power to destroy massively whatever man has built—including conceivably, though not probably, the recondite trails leading to those very discoveries. The era of "the civilizations" being past, what we now enter is either the era of civilization or the era of universal desolation. I shall write as though only the former alternative were before us; but I shall be writing of the conditions under which alone that alternative can be realized.

iv. *Extent of World-community: Danger of Unbalance*

WHAT is the extent, at present, of this common property?

As I have suggested, not all parts of a civilization spread with equal pace. Custom, happily, remains local; together with folklore and folk arts, and therewith the *Volksgeist* itself, in which Savigny rightly saw the genius of positive law. These all have universal ingredients, but also ingredients incurably local; they are not "clean universals." It is the abstract universal that most swiftly makes its way, the logic and mathematic, the commercial habits which in the nature of the case have to cross boundaries, so that commercial and maritime law are the earliest ingredients of a working *jus gentium.* Among technical devices, arts of agriculture spread more slowly than arts of metallurgy and mining. Political forms, having to link together past, present, and future of a persistent national group, cannot spread as easily as a turn of industrial artifice.

Nevertheless, there are no important political or legal ideas that are not today shelled out from their local wrappings and everywhere discussed as universal. Libraries of Buddhist monasteries, and even of the department stores of Tokyo prior to the war, commonly contained political classics in European languages, not omitting the works of Marx and Engels. The budding Civil Code of prewar China, as the codes of Japan and Siam at that time relatively new, was fully cognizant of earlier European and American codes. The Chinese code was especially alive to the universal aspect of a workable civil law; the preface to the first volume, *General Principles* (in English translation, Shanghai, 1930), refers to the elements of "juridical science which are now becoming world-wide," while indicating that the principles of the law of real property and of the family must retain Chinese localisms.

Partly because of the more rapid spread of the abstract universal, and partly because of the instinct of modernity for separation of distinguishable functions, the modern state everywhere tends to be the secular state, in Asia as well as in the West. And so far as this is the case, the new states of Asia inherit the problems which tend to enfeeble the secular state—as I pointed out earlier.

With this illustration in mind, I hazard the generalization that it is precisely because of the superior speed and penetrating power of the abstract universals that the coming civilization is threatened by an unbalance which may imperil its advent.

The claim of the East upon the universals of the West is invulnerable. It is supported by contributions from the Orient to fields of theory formerly considered the peculiar provinces of western minds. Fields which are essentially abstract, as mathematics and logic, raise no question of balance. Fields in which the universal is extracted from its setting, as in law or cosmology, may raise such question. Let me illustrate:

The theory of "rights" as a basis of law is one of the abstractions whose potential menace to the societies of its origin we have already noticed. It has nevertheless a universal trait which the nineteenth century has been unable, with the united denunciation of its leading schools of jurisprudence, wholly to repress. The new nation-states of our era, eastern as well as western, totalitarian as well as liberal, have been unable to escape at least lip service to the rights of the natural man. The elaborate Declaration made by United Nations was not addressed to democracies alone; and the Soviet Constitution of 1936 has a place for the idea.[4] It has been the pride of the modern state of the West that it can concede to its individual members the maximum of liberty and right without losing its coherence (a point which drew the admiring comment of Hegel, *Phil. des Rechts*, 75 n., presumably with England in mind). But just on this account, the maxim in question con-

---

[4] When the subcommission engaged in formulating this Declaration came to consider the "right to work," the Soviet delegate favored an unrestricted assertion of that right, whereas Mrs. Eleanor Roosevelt, in the chair of the subcommittee, demurred as representing the American view that economic conditions may not always allow everyone to be employed. The Soviet delegate urged that the Declaration must present not the actual but the right! The Soviet view prevailed. Today (1955) in the U.S.A. it is labor—i.e., organized labor—that contests the universality of the "right to work."

fesses having given the highest possible gage to the uncontrollable factor of individual morale. And the contemporary western individual is no longer the custom-and-conscience-borne person of John Locke, nor yet of Blackstone or Jefferson. He presents, as we have noted, a far wider political incalculability. And if this is true in lands still aware of traditional premodern intangibles of social control, what of lands whose intangibles arc far different?

And in both hemispheres today, this incalculability is increased by the swift persuasive force of an abstract universal in the field of cosmology, on which I have barely touched.

v. *Specter of the Purposeless Universe: Unique Exigency of Western Civilization becoming Universal*

IT BELONGS to the empirical conscience of modern science to relieve nature, not alone of all purpose in the shape of "final causes," but as well of all quality and value. If "nature" is synonymous with the cosmos, we men inhabit a universe purposeless and meaningless, a realm of fact and event ideally mathematical in process, ideally empty of choice. If this is indeed "the Real" with which we have to do, our human purposes find there no objective support. But Descartes, who on one side of his dualism has given us this purpose-purged world picture, is the same as he who on the other side has given us the sole certitude of the subjective I-think. May we then take refuge in our subjective being, claiming not only the "secondary qualities," but the entire realm of value as our own? Since values have no other source, they are "our kingdom"; they impose no obligation—we are free to make them as we will. Indeed, since there is nothing in the nature of things to steady our aim, we are foredoomed to this freedom; and if, as M. Sartre sees it, our value-setting decision tends—in strangely Kantian fashion—to universalize its maxim, it can be attended with the unique distress (Sartre's *angoisse*) of unguided responsibility.

But this same empirical conscience that provides the purposeless universe allows us no rest in value-setting subjectivity. For eventually it turns its searching light upon man himself as an object within nature: it creates a science of man, a psychology, a sociology, an anthropology. And since the human phenomenon cannot disavow the character of the whole, it, together with its value-setting activities, must share the resulting desiccation: value-setting is itself a product of valueless necessity.

Our modern self-awareness is thus confronted with two opposing versions of its own nature, each of which claims a certain necessity, while their co-existence presents an apparently insoluble enigma. Spinoza's effort to keep them both, while avoiding collision by the device of parallel time orders, fails to satisfy the claim of each to include all that is valid in the other. And neither of the two gives any basis for the notion of a right common to all men.

We cannot abandon our empirical conscience, and its consequences. The methods of a value-free science are genuine universals, however abstract. And this theory of human rights, renascent in the present century, becoming part of a world-wide political pattern, without the conceptions of human nature that once made democracy inwardly strong, can only contribute to its disintegration, and tend to dissolve the coming civilization even while we build it.

But we must look again at this scientific world picture
which is at the heart of at least part of the political embar-
rassment of our time, and which, like our individualism,
cannot be simply rejected. For this world picture has also
become an integral part of the entire contemporary civilization. The present moment is indeed one of widespread
revolt against what Fechner called the "night view" of
nature—that purposeless and qualityless cause-tight universe which a perfected science, including the sciences of
man, would insist upon. His classic statement deserves re-
reading, for its prophecy is fulfilled in our day. Its opening represents an experience of perhaps 1840, when he was
recovering from an eye malady which had compelled him
to give up his university post. I translate some of the
opening paragraphs:

> One morning I sat on a bench in the Leipzig Rosenthal in
> the neighborhood of the little Swiss chalet, and looked through
> an opening among the bushes over the wide and lovely meadow
> there spread out, in order to refresh my ailing eyes on its
> expanse of green. The sun was bright and warm . . . There
> were flowers . . . butterflies . . . birds . . .; and notes from
> a morning concert reached my ear. But for one accustomed to
> thinking, gradually upon this enjoyment of the senses a play
> of thought began to spin itself out. . . .
> Strange illusion, said I to myself. In reality is everything
> before me and around me Night and Silence; the sun that
> seems to me so blazing-bright that I refrain from turning my
> eyes to it, is in truth only a dark ball seeking its way in perfect
> gloom. The flowers, butterflies, deceive with their colors, the
> violins and flutes with their tones. In this universal darkness,
> desolation, silence engulfing heaven and earth, there are scat-
> tered beings, as it were (conscious) points, inwardly illumined,
> colored, sounding; they emerge from the night and sink back
> into it, without leaving anything behind of light and sound.

. . . So today, and so from the beginning, and so will it be forever. . . .

How could I come on such absurd thoughts? . . . They are the thoughts of the entire thinking world around me. However else they differ, in this, philosophers and physicists, Darwinians and Anti-Darwinians, orthodox and rationalists, reach each other the hand. This is not a building stone, it is *the foundation stone* of the contemporary world view.

This is the night view! And, as Fechner continues, "if the world had ever presented to itself the complete improbability, the entire weakness of the ground of this view as they came to me in that hour, it could never have become a world view."

And with this illumination—for it was such—Fechner finds complete confidence that as day succeeds night, so the day view will eventually succeed the night view.[5]

Certainly the purposeless universe is the negation in advance of all religion in the sense of a cosmic call to right living, or a rootage in the Real of man's subjective valuations.

Nevertheless, that night view is itself an achievement of the first magnitude. It is a conception made possible by the mathematical genius of modernity, and by the empirical honor of a host of scientific observers. The building of that corporate body of truth called science is a monumental accomplishment of thought disciplined by a relentless moral ideal. A godless world picture? Yes; unless, as Gandhi seemed to think, Truth is itself a god; for truth as an abiding and growing totality is certainly not a material structure. As a product of honor-governed thought the edifice of science can never be abandoned, even though the

[5] Gustav Theodor Fechner (1801–87), professor of physics in Leipzig, and the chief initiator of experimental and metrical psychology, was a thinker whose genius broke through the crust of then prevalent conceptions of nature founded on a Cartesian-Newtonian physics. In 1879 he published a small book called *The Day View over against the Night View (Die Tagesansicht gegenueber der Nachtansicht)* here quoted.

world it displays, devoid of inherent purpose, is inanimate, and in this sense a dead world.

Both in its value-purged structure and in its extent, it is a world in which man is lost. Hegel remarks of the Roman world that there for the first time the soul of man could be thoroughly lost. In our present immeasurably vaster world room of uncountable galaxies and unsayable time ranges—all indifferent to human fate—the lostness of the human soul attains a depth incomparably greater.

And note that this is an exigency no prior civilization has faced. Neither India nor Egypt nor China nor Greece had any conception of the dead world of astrophysics implied in the clear vision of Descartes. Karma has indeed an inexorable legality; but it is a legality sensitive to moral qualities, hence not possibly inanimate. In none of these earlier civilizations had the physical and the mental been sundered, still less the sense qualities of nature from the equationable qualities. For instance, a Chinese philosopher mentioned to me as a point of superiority the fact that China "had *no Descartes.*" Prior to our seventeenth century there had never been anywhere a "bifurcation of nature" such as Whitehead has well named and denounced, together with Goethe and Fechner. And this bifurcation is without doubt an unnatural malady. But unless this malady is experienced, the actual implications of scientific method have not been fully encountered. It is necessary to the soul's maturity that the thought of man should descend into this pit of the meaningless universe. If he is to be saved from that pit, his metaphysical insight, his religion, must descend with him.

And in point of fact, this his religion has already by anticipation done.

vi. *Religious Parentage of Night View:*
Purpose of the Purposeless

FOR if we rightly read the story of the genesis of modern science, and answer the question why its relentless logic appeared only in Europe, we shall see that it is the religion of Europe which begot the empirical conscience, and thus indirectly all its fruits. It is not an accident that Bacon in formulating the principle of empirical observation fell into a form of words recalling the fundamental paradox of Christian morals, "He that loseth his life for my sake shall find it." Bacon's words are, "We cannot command nature except by obeying her"—clearly the mental phase of that same paradox. It is the willful curbing of self-will which had been the discipline of Christian morals for a millennium and a half.[6] It was the purposeful exclusion of purpose from the field of theoretical physics that swung the door open to a universal science and technology.

Once we have traced this concept of the meaningless universe to its moral origins, we can begin to interpret its apparent threat. The original moral purpose is a purpose to "objectify." But it cannot objectify itself—it may *per contra* even forget itself; yet it cannot expunge itself from the world picture. The cause-tight character of that universe is a property, not of the whole but solely of what can be objectified and set into calculable group relations: the night view, then, valid for its own data, is an abstraction: it omits *quality*—yet quality is part of the fact; *consciousness*—yet consciousness is the condition of any value or "importance" whatever; *volition*—the response to meaning and truth—yet volition is *there*!

[6] I have commented on this parental relationship in *What Man Can Make of Man*, 26 f.

The night view, I say, is an abstraction; but it is a *necessary abstraction*. Necessary not alone for the community of scientific labor, but also because it is only the nonpurposive that purpose can be wholly free to utilize. It is only an inanimate world segment that can be exploited for human ends without consideration or compunction. If all actual being were conscious and purposive, plowing a field would be inflicting microscopic tragedies on an immense scale! Hence those who like Fechner and Whitehead seek to remedy the appalling vacuousness of nature's intricate fabric by a universal reanimation are, I fear, surrendering a genuine and world-changing human advance.

When it is once seen that the purpose of science cannot extrude purpose and value from an empirical account of the real, the essential step is taken; and the succeeding steps must preserve an equally rigorous economy of hypothesis. The purpose which has revealed the purposeless process *within nature* has for its goal, what? The goal of the explorer, who must climb Annapurna "because it is there"? Yes. The mapping of our finite situation within the endless wonder of fact? Yes. A fading hope of practical adjustments of human living to infinite contingency? Perhaps. But at least this: a recovery of proportion, of fearlessness toward the limitless inanimate, through some glimpse of the ulterior purpose of the simple existence of any island of purpose whatever. The progress of physical science has its own intrinsic joy of mastery—it needs no ulterior aim; but with the mastery implied in its powerful (and beautiful) equations, there is joined the anticipation of a further mastery of "understanding." And it is in this sense that "to master nature" we first yield to her our unreserved empirical "obedience."

For this reason, I can only with qualification follow Toynbee in his judgment that the modern period has rejected the guidance of religion in accepting the guidance of man-made science. Unless I am mistaken, the characteristic development of science in modern Europe is not only a corollary of the religion of Europe but in a significant sense part of that religion. Scientific empiricism is simply the constant and unreserved will to truth in yielding one's preconceptions and wishes to the evidence of fact and of the universal lawfulness embodied in event.

The vast defection of modernity is not that it has been scientific but that its science has been at critical points untruthful and therefore unscientific. Through excess of zeal and through forgetting the auspices of its own search for truth it has made or implied metaphysical assertions to which it has no right, such as that mathematical nature is the whole of reality, and that what empirical science can show of man is the whole of human nature. A scrupulous empiricism of the positivist type would refrain from any such implication. A wider empiricism shows both of these judgments false.

A truthful science will admit that in the strict sense of the term there is no science of man; there is science only of the manikin, the robot. Man embodies the duality of the world, the events which are his life flow both from reasons (including ends) and from causes; but they flow from causes only by the consent of his reasons. If he fails to eat he will die; but his instinctive eating is none the less an act of rational will. The life process of man is end-seeking, involving an organism of causes; it is definitely not one of causes excluding ends. And the end-seeking is a function of his interpretation of reality. In a living universe it may become a phase of love; and that love a participation in a purpose which is the final cause of the whole. On the validity of this interpretation, a truthful science passes no judgment.

But the untruthful science has permeated our incipient world civilization, and is especially deadly where the course of science has entered new ground. The vices of the West become the poison of the East, which has no acquired immunity. In the transmissions of culture, a new civilization frequently tends to borrow the perversities of the old; and in this present matter, the englobement of all world process and of human nature in the nexus of physical law, with the resulting secularization of all life, has a peculiar plausibility and sanction. The character of the ensuing stage of history will depend much on whether with this perversity there can go also the specific remedy already potentially present in the West.

vii. *Can the Religious Parent Meet the Emergency?*

THE immediate practical suggestion would appear to be that with the science should go the religion from which its method sprang, both in the West and in the East. This suggestion is significant, but only on two conditions: One, that Christianity in the West should recover its vitality, and reconceive its message, to the extent of meeting in its own house the malaise of its own offspring. Two, that Christianity can show itself universal and not "western," and therefore as belonging—with as good a claim as that of science—to all men, not as something borrowed or imported or imposed from outside, but as their own birthright.

These are questions to be pursued further.

STUDY IV*

CHRISTIANITY: ITS CHARACTER AND FUTURE ROLE

i. *Why Christianity? Its Special Responsibility*

WE ARE dealing with long-range alterations of civilization, in which, we may now assume, religion is somehow involved. In spite of the fact that all such long-range alterations take place without our leave and beyond all our planning, we can now recognize an incipient world civilization as being ushered in by certain interior necessities of the historical process—always by the leave of possible catastrophe from which we perforce abstract. The inherently universal elements of human culture have begun to be actually universal by spontaneous appropriation. The dimly unitary world situation thus created inherits from the earlier East and West unlosable elements, which, as they accumulate, tend to preserve the area won for common understanding.

Among these common properties are the specific advances which we in the West ascribe to "the modern era." With them is inherited also a liability to certain maladies definitely apparent in the West. The character of the for-

* Portions of Study IV appeared in *The Hibbert Journal*, July, 1956.

ward movement everywhere will depend on what is done, and first of all on what is thought, about these maladies. May we escape them by returning to the *status quo ante*? The postulate which launches the inquiry of the present Study is that, even if we would, *we cannot escape these ills by rejecting these advances*, as we are sometimes plausibly advised to do.

What these advances are, and what these perils, I need not here recapitulate. Yet—as with experience I have come to fear repetition far less than obscurity—allow me in the briefest terms to restate the main elements of our problem:

The advances are, first, the advance into a new degree of self-consciousness or subjectivity, which tends to ripen into relativism and psychologism. And second, the complementary advance into a new degree of objectivity, conveyed by the scientific method itself, which tends to ripen into the night view of Fechner and the stupendous vision of the purposeless universe. These gains are borne on the most swiftly convincing aspects of the modern outlook, those abstract universals which are inherently every man's property. Our science and technology, for example, require no foreign mission to promote them and call for no "thank you": they enter at once and by right into the fabric of whatever world segment catches their vision, and retaining their own identity everywhere, constitute immediately an element of world unity.

Whatever infirmities these ripenings may breed have their sources therefore in the genius of modernity itself. The factors of creative thought which have begotten the advances including presumably western religion, become co-responsible for the infirmities. And if the West on ac-

count of the tradition of Christianity has a partial prophylaxis against these ills, *its nature deserves an inquiry*. I say
prophylaxis rather than immunity; for it is precisely in
the western world that the ills have developed in their
most acute form. Christianity has neither prevented their
appearance nor cured them. Christianity, as it stands
today, has still a problem of coexistence with these advances and their results. And further, it does not transmit
itself with the same obvious universal right. It does indeed
claim, as must every valid religion, inherent universality;
and it seeks actual universality, chiefly from western
centers. But it moves with far greater resistance than the
swift-spreading abstractions of modernity, to which a
secular world view appears most germane; their advance,
so far from aiding the progress of Christianity, may appear as hostile to its very existence.

Especially the advance into objectivity, with its necessary elimination of the purposive factor from the theory
of the physical cosmos, presents itself as taking issue not
with Christianity in particular, but with religion in general. It opposes any view that declines to make "Nature"
a synonym for all there is. The enemy is supernature in
any form.

Yet Christianity is peculiarly involved. For it is not pure
accident that the Europe which alone became saturated
with Christianity is the same Europe which alone became
the breeding place of modernity—including "modern science." There is a parental relation between them becoming
slowly evident to historians, some phases of which we have
noticed.

The "I-think, I-exist" of Descartes had an obvious
paternity in St. Augustine. But so also, the first principles
of the empirical attitude which has become the mark of

the true scientist, and which forbids the intrusion of his personal wishes or predilections into the minutely responsible work of observation and experiment. There we have a definite moral background in two phases of the Christian tradition. First, as we have already noted (p. 60), in the precept of losing one's life in order to save it, as the prototype of Bacon's dictum that in order to master nature we must first obey her, a principle which involved the repudiation of the appeal to "final causes" as a reading of human motivation into natural event. Second, in the derivation of Kepler's later view of the true inwardness of physical processes: his *verae causae*, the genuine causes, as distinct from the fanciful or speculative causes which allowed the planetary motions, for example, to be guided by attendant spirits—these *verae causae* were homogeneous with the effects, or as a later mathematical concept would express it, the events which constitute nature are a closed group. This austerity of mathematical principle, he considered, was alone compatible with that world of perfect law which is God's thought, and whose beauty is at the same time its freedom from incongruous admixture. On this ground, he himself dismissed his planetary spirits as superfluous and inharmonious, and thus handed on to Galileo, Descartes, and Huygens the concept of an autonomous nature, cleared for the unhindered sweep of the equations of a new mathematical calculus.

Because of this parenthood, Christianity is committed as is no other religion to seek a place in its world view for what seems its contradiction, the lean and mind-swept system of nature that appears to follow from these premisses. Nature will be conceived, not with Spinoza as another name for God, but as self-operating without God's intrusion (*natura non sive Deus sed sine Deo*).

And so long as Christianity coexists with this autonomous, emancipated, secularized science of nature, modernity, uneasily entertaining both, though not in wholly identical groups, cannot be a single state of mind. It has enjoyed and enjoys a divided consciousness. If Christianity were able, on its own ground, to overcome this tension, through providing a world view of equal integrity and inclusive scope, it would be prepared to relieve various maladies of the present confused civilization not only in western lands, but also in the expanding world scope beset by the same quandaries.

Whether it can do so, as a religious interpretation of the human lot, factually responsible and inherently universal, is the theme of our present study.

ii. *The Tension as Reflected in Modern Philosophy*

WHERE neither of two opposing views is able to cancel the other over a considerable period of time—and where in spite of appearances neither is quite willing to do so because of a submerged sense of the existing family bond— the tension between them is likely to be the area of our best opportunity for deepening our understanding of both. Thus the long tension between Christianity and the insights of modernity promises—in view of our postulate— new and revealing light from some of the most familiar passages of history.

This tension has haunted the mind of man throughout the modern period. It was present from the beginning, as when after sharp discussion involving the Theological Faculty of the University of Leiden, in which city Descartes had brought out his maiden *Discours* and had carried out experiments in anatomy, his works were barred from university use. The issue was felt at once; yet it was phenomenally slow to find its accurate definition—if I am right, has only recently found it. Its battle was therefore fought on a variety of mistaken fronts—especially from the religious side as a warfare against science in general and from the scientific side as a contest against "final causes" in general. It was fought through all pertinent channels— through literature, poetry, graphic art, politics —as well as through philosophy. But it is in the broad lines of philosophical effort, as in its nature the interpreter between human intuition and the sharpening techniques of reason, that we can best see the meaning and changing fortunes of the struggle.

Once Descartes had defined his two loci of certitude— for he had two, the I-exist and the mathematical rigor of nature's processes—the way was invitingly open to set up a system, either of pure objectivism (as of Hobbes) or of pure subjectivism (as of Malebranche and Berkeley). But the major thought works of the early era, those of Locke, Spinoza, and Leibniz, arose from an unwillingness to abandon either aspect, or to reduce one to the other. Each held firmly to what he considered the scientific enlightenment; each held in his own way to the realities of thought and feeling, and to a ruling Reality within which man's moral being can find a home.

The same is true of later speculative efforts, those of Kant and Hegel, those also of the present century with its recovered courage of metaphysical synthesis—Royce, Bergson, Whitehead: all of these arise from an unwillingness to surrender either aspect of the dilemma.

This unwillingness, most marked in the philosopher-scientists—Leibniz, Newton, Kant—to whom the mathematical vision continued to hold a religious aura, was

shared from the side of Christianity as it gained a grasp of
its new responsibilities. It became unwilling to maintain
opposition to the findings of an empirical conscience which
itself had nursed into existence.[1] With this growing perception of its own stake in the majestic growth of the
edifice of scientific truth, the "warfare between science and
religion" ceased to resound. Where can anything deserv-
ing that name be found today?

Religion must in any case hold to its fundamental conviction that nature is neither the whole nor self-explana-
tory. But Christianity has not been content with dogmatic
inflexibility. It has labored—no doubt with much groaning
—to incorporate into its world view the cosmological picture being drawn trait by trait by the developing sciences,
evolution and all! It now rests its own case on solider
ground than that of arbitrary intervention, the exceptional, the miraculous—namely, on the completer truth of
experience. "Empiricism" is not the name of its enemy
unless empiricism is mounted, as positivism has attempted,
on the vanishing knife edge of "the given," the ideal "sense
datum" from which all thought, all interpretation, all
meaning is banished—that is to say, on the meaningless.[2]
The broader empiricism, with which alone a consistent
science can operate, the empiricism of meaning, of Husserl's *Wesensschau*, of the universal, is the potential friend
of religion, debouching as we have seen in the empiricism
of intersubjectivity. Here Christianity is at home.

At the same time, it may firmly call on the secular outlook to disavow its unscientific pronouncements in the field

---

[1] *Op. cit.*, 25.

[2] "*L'empirisme en tant que philosophie de l'immédiat se detruit lui-
meme; l'immédiat est l'inverse d'un principe d'intelligibilité.*" Marcel,
Journal Métaphysique, 3. Cf. also *Husserliana*, I, 19: "*nicht ein blosser
Zusammenhang von Daten. . . .*"

of metaphysical negation—as that nothing exists but "nature"—physical nature; and that in the ultimate analysis the world of the night view, the mindless world, is the original and the surviving reality when the episode of consciousness and human ideals is obliterated in the relentless entropy of available potential energy. This prospect of final despair which, as Bertrand Russell estimates the scene, is as nearly certain as any unprejudiced reason can judge, our secular view must acknowledge as a half-truth, not the whole—an abstraction, not an ontology.

Thus reconceiving its own bases of strength, Christianity need be no longer a timorous rear guard, retreating with every advance of science. It may become a Christianity self-aware in presence of a human need that increases, not diminishes, with that advance and with every humanistic step toward tangible as well as mental self-sufficiency.

Throughout this entire three-century period of encounter with the objective conscience of modern science, Christianity has also experienced an eventful interaction with modern subjectivity.

It was in the nature of things that the firm certitude of the Cartesian I-think should present itself as a triumph of the spirit over matter, a guarantee of the soul's immortality, a refuge from the mechanical, a substantial basis for the demand for justice to the individual person, whose rights Christianity had espoused from the beginning. The explicit idealisms of Leibniz and Berkeley, and also the implicit idealisms of Locke and Grotius in the field of law, embodying these fruits of the subjective advance, tended to confirm the general religious outlook, and were in turn confirmed by that outlook. Christianity recognized—as in Malebranche—a philosophical *rapprochement*.

The subjective principle needed criticism and received it freely, both within and without the philosophical current. Yet the inescapable I-think which absorbs "all my representations" entered heavily into subsequent thought systems, even those seeking to escape it. This I-think is present in, and sustains, not only the later idealisms from Kant to Bradley, Bosanquet, Royce, but also the pragmatisms of James and Dewey, the operationalisms of postrelativity physics (as with Bridgman), and at various points the speculations of Russell and the majestic synthesis of Whitehead.[3]

It is not strange that Christian theology—if only on the broad platform that "Spirit creates and governs the

---

[3] Most explicitly in his "repudiation of the notion of vacuous actuality" (*Process and Reality*, viii, 43, etc.), meaning thereby his denial that any real thing can be devoid of consciousness or some lesser grade of "subjective immediacy": every real entity has inner self-feeling as its center of being. Whitehead is much exercised to keep this subjective factor in place. Philosophy "is the self-correction by consciousness of its own initial excess of subjectivity" (22). In *Science and the Modern World* he denounces "subjectivism" in the sense of the belief that "the world is in me": in *Process and Reality* he devotes an entire chapter to the theme (Pt. II, ch. VII). Yet in his "Two Lectures on Life and Nature" at Chicago, he agrees that both propositions, "I am in the world" and "The world is in me," have their meed of validity. And his theory of "prehensions," as a modified version of Bacon's suggestion that in nature things "apprehend" each other, is (as I understand it) a complete rejection of the physicalist theory of perception (P. & R. viii).

Husserl, in his most revealing essay, *Cartesian Meditations,* now published in his original German script as *Die Pariser Vorträge*, has a similar in-and-out relation to the omnivorous I-think. The "intentionality" which gives my experience universality is itself, he holds, still a private affair: *"Alle Scheidungen, die ich mache zwischen echter und trügender Erfahrung und in ihr zwischen Sein und Schein, verlaufen in meiner Bewusstseinssphäre selbst. . . ."* And in the end, though he fights to overcome solipsism, he fails to throw off the ever-recurring net of the monadic vision. His *"monadologische Intersubjectivität"* fails of being a thorough intersubjectivity, because he bases it only on the consubjectivity of fellow monads, and not on the intersubjectivity of the universal Thou-art (*Husserliana* I, 31, 121 ff.).

world"—has at times inclined to affiliate itself with some variant of idealism.

But Christianity was bound to find idealism a broken reed, as idealism was through the nineteenth century, an idealism incompletely freed from the solipsistic taint. Since the first obligation of religion is to unite the individual self with the real as Other Self, Christianity could have no durable commitment to a scheme of thought whose absolute Thou-art remains a subjective postulate, or an object of feeling, or if found in history tends to disappear in a cultural mist, whether Hegelian, anthropological, or social-historical. Until modern philosophy had found its own solution of the dilemma, it was in the nature of things that Christianity should pass through a period of concern to cleanse its skirts of "idealism."

But this period of purification has done its work with less than clear perception of the issue. The rejection of an undefined "idealism," fallaciously identified with the subjective principle itself, loses sight of an unyielding necessity in all religion—that the clean aloneness of the subjective I-am, free from social involvement, must be the starting point of all religious experience, the measure of its depth and vitality. Religious experience as a personal concern is "the redemption of solitude": the individual "is not a mystic until his own spirit has made its solitary leap to God, like a tongue of flame out of the midst of the fire." [4] The present indiscriminate—almost fashionable—repudiation of idealism by theology, granting its due grounds, not only loses a factor of immense power in the spirit of modernity, but stands to lose the path through which philosophy has already remedied the defect and holds faith with *both advances* of modernity.

[4] *The Meaning of God,* 402–4.

What that path is we have already roughly traced.[5] In the guise of a "synthesis of idealism and realism" it has long been a philosophic ambition. The "objective" and "absolute" idealists following Kant were moved by it; the later Schelling attempted it with some success. But the solving deed could not occur until philosophy was once more as much at home with the spirit of science and with its technical instruments as it was in the seventeenth and eighteenth centuries. With Fechner, Lotze, Poincaré, and Royce, philosophy once more entered this avenue; Charles Peirce had glimpses of the way in which a solution must come; Whitehead has assumed a gigantic labor of reconstruction; and a generation of physicists, including Max Planck, Nils Bohr, Heisenberg, and C. F. v. Weizsaecker, has joined hands with philosophy in the task, which becomes necessarily co-operative.

But the decisive step has required something more, and something less, than a full absorption of scientific technique; namely, a deeper analysis of the empirical principle itself such as we have indicated. And merging with this work, one current of philosophical inquiry, at points in touch with religious thought, has followed an independent and devious path which has for us a special interest because, instead of repudiating subjectivism, it has taken the unpromising road of an even more radical subjectivity. By its unbridled and various nature it throws a vivid light upon the quandary of our philosophical position, and on the relation of Christianity thereto. It will reward a look.

It originates—about the 1840's—in a valiant dialectical attempt to dethrone dialectic—the polemic of Kierkegaard

[5] Above, pp. 30 *et seq.*

against Hegel in the interest of the most inward crisis of the individual soul.

The root of Kierkegaard's passionate concern for the anxious world peril of the solitary self—first of all his own self, yet as with Descartes conceived defiantly as the universal plight of man—lay long dormant. It slept beneath the noise of a kindred passion, professedly anti-Christian —Nietzsche's violent gospel of man-generating-the-beyond-man by inflicting surgery on himself: *Geist ist das Leben, das selber ins Leben schneidet.* Reviving the old root, and still in the spirit of that self-overcoming *Geist,* a philosophy called Existentialism has been casting unordered shafts of light into the darkness of human existence and destiny, leaving them for the most part in sharper darkness because of the shattered and defeated light.

The common element in this willfully branching movement lies in finding within the I-exist a depth of meaning which the impoverished dictionary sense of "existing" or "being" (and its terminal position at the tiptop of Porphyry's tree) seems to forbid. It reminds us that our existence, definable or not, gets less tangible meaning point-blank than from a contrast, its contrast with a thinkable and *possible nonexistence.* My being borders on my nonbeing at every angle. And as I peer into the bottomless gulf of my nonbeing, I realize that it lies always within the scope of my freedom to step off—into nothingness. All the passion with which my will-to-live is freighted crowds itself into the narrow, fragile, arbitrary, perhaps indefensible fact, I exist: at least *my* whole world is in it. Of a sudden the emptiest of concepts becomes the fullest; existence becomes *Existenz,* passion-charged being.

A solitary reflection! A solitary concern? The almost

whimsical all-importance of this to-be-or-not-to-be I have
no choice but to impute to every I-exist in the universe: my
privatest anxiety is every man's. And were all such to
exercise at once their freedom not to be, would any meaning be left in the universe? [6] *Existenz*, necessarily private-
personal, becomes momentous, the one truly momentous
thing in the world. More intensely than for Descartes, the
I-exist declares itself a necessary beginning for philosophy
—subjectivity to the extreme limit, not of thought alone
but of passion as well. Perhaps one must add that, far less
than Descartes, does Existentialism as a whole—if it is a
whole—know what to do with this beginning.

Among the representatives of this trend,[7] it is Gabriel
Marcel who has most perceptively pursued its logic to a
solution—though with deliberate rejection of "system"—
and also to an understanding of his own with Christian
tradition. He has done so first in a personal journal (*Journal Métaphysique*, 1927), relating a mental journey that
traverses the full length of the idealist thread in modern
philosophy with which in earlier years he had been deeply
engaged. This with later works contains the story of his
emancipation from this idealism ("within an idealistic
frame," he is careful to note), an emancipation helped by
his studies with Bergson, and by other phases of that wider
empiricism whose outlines we have traced. And he reaches
—as most Existentialism does not—the crucial perception
of an intersubjectivity in which the objective and subjective insights of modernity are preserved and cured. In him

[6] Heidegger, *Sein und Zeit*; Helmut Kuhn, *Encounter with Nothingness*. It is apparent that at this point Existentialism is tangent to the
insight of Fechner above referred to p. 57), a contemporary of Kierkegaard.

[7] Though like others of scrupulous conscience, Marcel is now inclined
to disavow identification with so ambiguous a movement.

alone, of this trend, the subjective experiment comes full circle and reaches inner coherence.[8] At the same time— and this is his special pertinence to the antisubjective issue —Marcel has made it I might almost say his crusade to preserve the clear essence of selfhood in its privacy and freedom from the grasp of technological objectivity and the pressures of a functional social milieu.[9]

Through Marcel, and through Etienne Gilson, who standing apart from Existentialism as a movement yet embraces its issues with a discerning sympathy, finding in Thomas Aquinas anticipation of *Existenz*, in the concrete and living sense of the notion of being-as-act,[10] this movement substantially promotes a reconception of Christianity pointing beyond the limits of the modern era, preserving it from an ultimately devastating antisubjectivism.

Nor must it be forgotten that the movement contains an

[8] See my article above cited, "Marcel and the Ground Issues of Metaphysics," 446 f. and 451–60. Sartre does on occasion assert that the awareness of self and of other-self are interdependent (as in *L'Existentialisme est un Humanisme*), yet his theory of *angoisse* appears to deny this insight.

[9] See his *Introduction to Journal Métaphysique*, xi: "*La position que j'ai cherchée à définir . . . consiste en effet à destituer la vérité de cette valeur d'au-delà qu'un certain rationalisme automatiquement lui confère—et du même coup à rèndre à l'existènce cette priorité métaphysique dont l'idéalisme a prétendu la priver. A cette égard, la distinction de l'existènce et de l'objectivité présente selon moi une importance impossible à exagérer.*" In brief, the real is not "*au-delà,*" but within experience; and the empirical is, at the same time, not swallowed up in the privacy of the I-think, nor the I-think in the observable otherness of the scientific "object." See also his much later work, now done into English as *Man and Mass Society.*

[10] In his recent book, *Being and Some Philosophers,* Gilson points out that St. Thomas, in regarding God as the author of existence, declares this gift of existence to be the gift of a power of action. To exist, for human beings, is to act as efficient causes; hence we may speak of the *act of existing,* of *esse* as a verb-active rather than of *ens* as formal presence-in-being. This insight certainly enters into the notion of *Existenz,* in which also we find the tensions of cosmic concern, and of what Marcel fitly terms *exigence.*

equally vigorous rejection of *antiobjectivity*, although, lacking the insight that could fuse these two demands, it has split on this point. As I know from what I have seen and felt, the power of this movement with the youth of a continent devastated by World War II, as well as with a wider public, lay largely in an uncompromising realism whereby the world revealed by science and hard fact is taken without demand for comfort, and without surrender of the I-will that goes with the I-think. The refuge for the stark objectivists, such as Sartre, was in no cosmic Thou-art, but in the power of an absolute freedom-in-self to shape and universalize its own values.

There is a dramatic excess in Sartre's version of freedom; its defiant Titanism proposing man as unlimited self-maker made-by-nothing stands in impossible contrast to the entities and events of nature, each made what it is by all the rest, hence wholly dependent and unfree. Man also is created; not self-evoked from Naught. But created man becomes man-the-creator; and what he is, as created being, contains his power-to-create. This, his radical freedom, can only be measured against the full unfreedom of the cause-tight mesh of physical nature. To this extent, the freedom and power of self-making pictured by Sartre belong to the full truth into which we must grow.

And that unfreedom against which it is measured must be retained with it: the phase of truth out of which the night view appears to emerge is as little abandonable as is the subjective advance. The two roots of modernity's malaise belong together, not as dead but as living and complementary—an aspect of that "principle of complementarity" through which Nils Bohr has proposed to unite the quantum and the wave, both of which enter into the constitution of radiant energy. It is only in their due union that there can be a working remedy for the ills of both abstractions.

How this union has been reached in the present century from the philosophical side, I have already indicated in bare outline. And this solution may guide us as we further inquire how the union may be reached from the side of religion.

I am far from proposing that it is primarily through philosophy that Christianity meets the issues presented by modernity. Philosophy is but a rude and remote indicator of the secret struggles of countless human souls carrying on the query-laden enterprise of living under existing conditions. Religion meets these struggles directly. But the philosophy that lives, lives only because those who struggle find it helpfully interpreting that struggle. It is not something apart from religion—it is an organ of the human thought without which religion is but a blind survival impulse, sometimes usurping the name of "faith"—which is never blind. Christianity, holding itself duly independent of philosophy (and on occasion unduly despising it), [11] has no choice but to come to terms with the concepts which the time spirit finds expressive of its own groping for light.

We may justly conclude therefore that in terms of the specific issues raised by modernity's "bifurcation of nature" the Christianity of the West has been actively reconceiving its own ground, taking a hesitant but promising part in the total movement of thought *beyond modernity*. It is thus approaching a fitness to meet universally the universal sources of disease. But since the experience and thought leading to this self-revision are chiefly western

[11] As in Reinhold Niebuhr's *The Self and the Dramas of History*, ch. XII *et seq.*

experience and thought, the question may still be raised, Is
Christianity universal? Or is it deepened in its westernism
by this very struggle?

We must give this question its full scope and careful
definition.

iii. *Christianity's Involvement in Western Life*

A RELIGION is always more than a scheme of thought.
And though usually less than an ideology, it is involved
with the whole organism of the culture it animates. Western
religion has, for over three centuries, had the unique advantage of constant intercourse with a science and a philosophical activity independent of itself, and yet relevant to
its being. Largely through this free intercourse it has
moved toward solving insights which, made part of its own
vital impulse, promise to give it curative impact on any
modern society. Yet this whole historic process, and its involvement in western culture, may tend to localize it. And
if Christianity as a whole is distinctively western, its significance for world civilization is—I will not say nullified from
the start, but discounted.

And not alone for the Orient. For western man is no
more capable than eastern man of accepting a religion
localized as western. What every man knows is that religion
is and has to be cosmic business, not hemispherical nor
otherwise limited in its competence to interpret and to
address the God of all mankind.

The day of private and local religions is over. It is over
by almost general consent—except as their history has
furnished special vessels for national feeling, of which I
shall have more to say. What we see now as local religions
are so, for the most part, only because the world has grown
up around their original spheres then considered total.

They now tend to break out of these domains. Hinduism has its missionary Vedanta; Islam has its Ahmadiyya; even Shinto has (or had) its Tenrikyo with a mission to California! Jealous gods and chosen peoples are normal chiefly within an accepted polytheism no longer thinkable.

The original proponents of a religious insight may fairly consider themselves "chosen," as holders of a "deposit of faith" defining a historic mission. Churches of a divinely ordained and continued episcopate incline to establish boundaries of acceptance similar in principle and effect, as establishing inner criteria lacking to an indiscriminate universalism. But the "chosen" in this sense are chosen to cancel their own chosenness through the spread of their own insight to all men. The good faith of chosenness is thus that it banishes its own distinction: hugged to itself it becomes an ally of religious *hybris* and corruption.

It remains true that religion—never an abstract universal—has to involve the whole man in his existing engagement with a historic community. It must address itself to the universal plight of the human soul; but the actual individual has to recognize his own personal plight in that universal description. The local experience of the specific community will paint itself into those terms. If Buddha addresses mankind as suffering, each Indian listener must needs read his own Indian suffering into the sermon: if a religion of Law addresses men as sinners, each one must find his own sense of sin, or lose the point of the appeal. If there are whole communities or whole peoples who have no "sense of sin" or find such a sense hard to acquire (we recall Vivekananda's striking cry before the Parliament of Religions in 1893: " 'Sinners'! It is a sin to call men sinners!")—a religion whose mission is to "save sinners" cannot be psychologically universal without first making universal the moral exigency to which it ministers. A religion can hardly escape being qualified by the world-and-self intuitions of the people through which it has developed.

If, then, Christianity and western civilization have grown up together, the universality of its terms—if they are universal—will not wholly relieve it from provincial coloring. We must therefore look beyond the sphere of philosophical and scientific problem-setting, and consider it in its broad relation to western history and experience.

Christianity and western civilization have indeed grown up together. It is perhaps fair to say that there is no phase of western culture that has not been nursed by this religion into a renewal of life after the Dark-Age period of confusion. We have taken the birth of scientific method as typical, though it is among the latest. We might have taken law, education, the family, forms of property, architecture, engineering, music . . . Here, as elsewhere in the world, all of these arts have borne marks of their religious parentage, and religious expression has been modified by occupation with these arts.

But here more than elsewhere, all these arts have revolted from the maternal domination. As definable spheres of interest "for their own sakes," they have rejected the ecclesiastical restriction. And here more than elsewhere this emancipation has been fairly complete, and has been a signal for new life, fertility, invention. And with this, a discovery of their own independent principles of being, as "secular" arts, strengthening and being strengthened by the secular outlook of the modern age. If this freedom means finding a more universal voice, it is possible that the local peculiarity of westernism in these fields is its approach to the intrinsically universal!

We must, however, add that here, as nowhere else, the
rill of creative liberty, cut off from the motive spring of
world passion in which every art is born, has tended to
run out into shallow artefact: something essential has been
lost. But meanwhile—and this is what here concerns us—
through their new-won autonomy the secularized arts have
rendered the religion signal service by their criticism from
the standpoint of their discovered light.

Science has done its share, as we observed, in bringing
religion to trim away elements of superstition, and to
transmute into metaphor and poetry certain indispensable
items of myth and imagination which as dogma clash with
the free course of legitimate science. Civil law has sobered
and humanized canon law. The humanist conscience has
co-operated with the Christian conscience first to define,
then to correct and curb, a legally workable doctrine of
human rights. The freed fine arts have found new materials, new techniques, new instruments, and withal new
principles—in some points reaching out to a community
of meaning with the fine arts of all lands.

Just to the degree in which these spheres of culture have
found universality through their independence, western
civilization in ceasing to be specifically Christian has also
ceased to be specifically western, and to that extent has
aided Christianity itself to divest itself of provincialism. In
so far as each art finds its own *lingua franca*, and in so far
as literature, without losing its spice of identifiable idiosyn-
crasy, becomes in Goethe's sense world literature, religion
cannot fail to discover its own art of speaking its message
to mankind in terms of a human, not western, psychology.

I say "in so far"; and the qualification is necessary. The
independence of the arts has not infallibly meant the discovery of the universal. Freedom from churchly limitations

has sometimes meant discovery of standards, sometimes the rejection of all standards, trying to live experimentally with none at all! It has here and there misjudged self-ruling as an invitation to self-norming, and has thus blinded itself to the sense of its own message to mankind. It is just the universal that is in danger of being lost; and western civilization, suffering under an exaggerated self-trust amounting to a worship of man-unleashed, cracks. Freedom is not enough; and, as Toynbee asserts, repentance is due. Without standard, no art, no right, no truth, no joy in living, no civilization to transmit! And without passion, no standard. The free arts must in some sense retain or regain their rootage in the universal as passion, i.e., in religion.

But does this mean a return to Christianity? Or has the revision of Christianity under the critiques of its own emancipated offspring—guided and misguided—has this incessant work of reconception brought Christianity to a simple coincidence with the general idea of religion, from which the accidents of its own history fall away? The total effect of its western experience would be, in that case, the emergence of the essential divested of the local—the achievement of its history *the overcoming of history.* If we hesitate to accept this result, do we not confess that, with all the clarification of its essential certitudes, Christianity remains western, while the West has largely ceased to be Christian?

The argument is impressive. It calls a response from all our hopes for purity and simplicity in whatever constitutes the institutional embodiment of our idea of the holy; from all within us that rebels against the complexities of dogma, the venalities of organization, and the intricate dust-covered treasures of the supernatural garret. Yet it harbors a fallacy.

I find that fallacy most clearly understood through the analogy of positive law; for law, like religion, has its universals which through history work toward clarification and power, as toward an ideal that would make a history of law—not superfluous, but as nearly unnecessary to the understanding of law as the history of mathematics is to the understanding of mathematics. But positive law, while accepting the ideal of inner universality, cannot shed its history: like every product of a growing life, it bears its history in itself. So a positive religion. When we recover from the reverse superstition, to the effect that an eternal truth, an *a priori* principle perhaps, must in the nature of the case be *always known*; when we recognize that the eternal truths, especially those of practical reason, have to have their human discoverers, announcers, messengers, hence their birthdays and the ups-and-downs of their applications, their eventful careers; we understand that the *vision of the eternal*—not the eternal itself—*must have its history.* And this history, in its own nature, tends rather to illustrate than to obstruct or distort the nature of the "principle" thus embodied. The issue is not whether Christianity can put off its history, its western involvement; it is whether with this its inescapable biography, it can so present the valid essences of religion as to give them unimpeded force, able to meet the issues created everywhere by the abstract universals of the secularized arts and sciences.

One test of this requirement is the test of simplicity; for the simple is not an empty unity devoid of detail, it is a unity declaring its power to integrate complexity. What we have to ask of Christianity is whether it is thus simplified, purged, disciplined—qualified by its own bitter

ordeal to descend into the pits dug for mankind by its own
followers, and to save them there. Something like this was,
I believe, the purport of a remark by Hu Shih, as we talked
together one March day in 1932, in the hospital of Peking
Union Medical College, where we happened both to be
casual patients. Hu Shih, not disposed to specific religion,
remarked objectively of Christianity that it was "relatively simple and pure." He meant, I think, that it had—as
a factor in Chinese life at that time—learned to emphasize
a few things as essential; and that it was comparatively free
from what Father Doré called *Les Superstitions Chinoises*,
and from the abuses of the prevailing "funeral rackets."
It was, he agreed, a westernizing influence, weaning many
of its followers too much away from sympathy with the
traditions, and from concern with the then current issues,
of Chinese life; but he considered—I think with much
magnanimity—that the deflection was temporary and un-
important as compared with the clarifying and motivating
of young Chinese minds, and that "they would find their
way back." Hu Shih was a wise enough judge of human
nature to know that ideas, even the simplest and truest, do
not work in a vacuum.

But whether Christianity is in fact prepared to meet the
coming civilization as clarified messenger of the universal,
this we cannot answer by assuming that we are ourselves
clear and at one as to what the essence of Christianity is.
We must again inquire, What is Christianity?

iv. *What Christianity Is*

THE recurrent quest for the "essence of Christianity"
must not overlook the fact that the original Gospel is already an essence, and proclaims itself as such. I venture to

*that which makes
something what
it is — fundamental
nature*

say that among sacred books the Christian scriptures are unique for the pervasive spirit of *induction*, announcing a single generating principle (or essence) from which the various items of a complex long-growing tradition can be deduced.[12] The Golden Rule, for example, is expressly announced as such an induction, "for this *is* the law and the prophets." The profound impact of the message of Jesus was due in no small measure to the masterful way in which earlier rules and doctrines were thus caught up in an essential simplicity, and illuminated thereby.

Now a powerful induction is no result of following logical rules—*pace* the textbooks, there are no rules! It comes as a stroke of insight, after long thoughtful mulling over the data, which—under new light from God knows where, probably an intimation of necessity—reconceives those data. The teaching of Jesus as a whole is an inductive reconception of the faith of the Hebrew lawgivers, prophets, and poets. I say "reconception" because his inductions at once integrate the tradition and extend it, not hesitating to correct points of tradition that deviate from the discerned principle, nor to rebuke a blind literalism in following the letter of the law; and doing this confidently, "as one having authority," because the grasp of essence admits for the first time an entrance into what the tradition really means. If the Teacher was right, he was the *first to understand Judaism* as well as to exemplify its meaning

[12] Buddhism as a reform of Brahmanism is less an induction from the earlier teaching than an original experiment in deviation. It does indeed appeal to broad characters of human experience, and to reason; its opening announcements are inductive generalizations not from the old rules but from the human lot, pointing out the pervasiveness of suffering in a sense not wholly alien to that of the Existentialists. The Buddha made no attempt to bring the Fourfold Truth or the Eightfold Path to a single principle, unless the "middle path" is such a principle. His appeal, however, is everywhere to the reflection as well as to the experience of his hearers. *Living Religions and a World Faith,* 94 f.

—in this sense to fulfill it—and also to go beyond it in applying its own principle, as the law of love in his hands goes beyond the rule of justice.[13]

Let us examine certain instances of this inductive relation of new to old at close range.

Teachings of Jesus as inductions. The Golden Rule is in some sense a commonplace of early ethical thought in various cultures. It is set apart, in the teaching before us, partly by its affirmative form which taken literally puts it beyond all possible observance, and partly by the comprehensive claim that in this form it can summarize the rest of the law. The common rule of reciprocity, the injunction to put oneself in the place of the recipient of one's act, stands, I think always, as one precept among many. As an induction summarizing the whole law, the golden rule takes place in the field of morals with the second and third of those universal principles of natural law, which Justinian adopts from Ulpian, *honeste vivere, neminem laedere, cuique suum tribuere*—live honorably, harm no one, render everyone his due; but with the ethical addition of initiative good will.

The Golden Rule is a precept for action. More characteristic of Christianity is the precept for feeling, "Thou shalt love God and neighbor," appearing in Leviticus among many items, here singled out as the master key, an essence. This precept of love would contain the Golden Rule as a corollary—it is a wider induction. But as a rule for feeling it appears to call for another impossibility—control of the uncontrollable: for who can regulate at will his loving or not-loving?

---

[13] And in another context the law of Tao beyond the rule of Jen, benevolence. Cf. Tao Teh King 38.

As an aspiring teacher of ethics in years long gone by, I was once reminded by a student, "You cannot *prove* that a man ought to love his neighbor; and if you could prove it, that would not in the least help him to do so." The thrust was keen.[14] Nevertheless, just for this reason it illuminates the leverage of the new teaching: this teaching assumes throughout that feeling is a proper object of religion's requirement, that man is free to "set his affections" where they ought to be set![15]

With the same radical courage of inward requirement, the Sermon on the Mount is addressed directly to the desires of the heart, with a specific requirement for each of the elemental impulses, acquisition, lust, pugnacity, not

[14] The sequel was even keener, and perhaps as relevant to the present discussion "I can understand," he went on to say, "how a Jesus Christ or a Nietzsche could turn the world upside down. But I cannot understand how a college professor could turn the world upside down." This was strong language, especially for the young Jew who so objectively assessed these world-changers. But he was essentially right: it is precisely the business of a religion to turn the world upside down, by making revolutionary demands on motivation that have to be made, leaving the question of practicability to the subject and the higher powers. And Nietzsche, who proposed to transvalue all values in the reverse direction, entered the lists with Jesus Christ in the field of religion. He thought he was opposing Christian slave morality; but he was, in fact, opposing a dry rot of Christian morale whose correction in due time will fortify the conception of Christianity. See below, p. 94.

[15] A far-off anticipation of what is today just dawning on politics and industry that it is not enough to *do* what you have to do—you must do it "and *like it*"! Otherwise you don't really do it—a distinct renunciation of behaviorism, also of Kant's view that law can ignore motivation, and of Spencer's dictum, "We can do as we please—we cannot do anything else—but we cannot please as we please."

Now a political requirement to enthuse, when you do not enthuse, like a conventional requirement to be amiable when you are not amiable, can be the most painful of infringements on human freedom, suitable only to the totalitarian conceptions of the scope of government. It is only in religion that a demand to love can be in order, and a failure to love be deemed a sin; for these standards are first of all standards for self-judgment, not for the police court.

as actions but as wishes. And it culminates in a summary, itself an induction unifying these several demands, "Be ye therefore perfect," leaving the impression that the Teacher, fully aware that his precepts were exceeding the possibilities of poor human nature, was also aware that as Teacher he could do no other than speak for the full requirement which that same human nature in quiet clarity must hold over itself. For to have any standard, and to have a standard of perfection in that field, are not two things but one.

This intention of the Teacher is implied in another summary precept which, calling for a further impossibility, seems to recognize the prior impossibilities: "Ye must be born again." For by some spiritual rebirth, and only thereby, could one's disposition-of-feeling so far change as to rise to the love of one's enemies, or to that distinctively Christian summons to forgiveness, which like the "perfection" attributed in the Sermon to the Heavenly Father refuses to follow the line of legal justice—forgiveness being definable as a will to be unjust in order, by eliciting a new temper in the case, to achieve a deeper justice. Here the Teacher deliberately enters the field of moral paradox, a field which had remained closed to all but the greater mystics.

And as if to bring together his own several inductions within a master induction, which is also a paradox, we have the dictum, "He that loseth his life for my sake, the same shall save it." In this expression, the words "for my sake" indicate an essential factor of the thought; namely, the affirmative power of a purposeful devotion, without which the blank formula "Die to live" gropes for foothold in the will. So understood, this precept can contain the others. Love itself is a losing of the life of the sole-self within the

life of another and completer self, and in that loss finding
realization.

Does this far-reaching induction, then, cover the whole
of the ethical code of Christianity? It brings to a focus the
sense of the new teaching, its element of rebuke to the
residual worldliness of the older codes, its radical demand
to "forsake all and follow me." But further, it joins direction with much of the moral aspiration of mankind in and
beyond the Jewish tradition. Do we not find human nature
struggling everywhere with the complementary paradox
that self-assertion—having the full sanction of natural
impulse—is self-defeating? And in the special instance of
requiting evil with good—which is losing the pugnacious
self in order to find it—we have the words of Plato and of
Lao Tze, Lao Tze adding the reason "that good may be
created." We may fairly ask whether the Teacher has not,
in this precept, offered an interpretation not only of the
essence toward which Judaism was striving, but of a universal striving of mankind. This universal striving we
might call [16] a striving beyond sole-selfhood and its nature-
defined desires, an inescapable awareness that the assertive
will fastens upon the asserter something less than the
wholeness of being to which he is called.

We shall for the moment leave this as a question. For the
Teacher, speaking in paradox, offers no total guide to life.
The "struggle for existence" had not raised its imperative
head so impressive to later centuries; the economic problem, whether for self or neighbor, is not solved by simple
neglect; and the content of that greater will in which self-
will is to be sublimated is left undefined, except in the
sweeping phrase "Seek ye first the Kingdom of God."

[16] With Robert Ulich, a striving for self-transcendence: *The Human
Career*, 1955.

Fulfillment of code requiring world view: faith and experience. But a religion is, in any case, something more than a code of morals. Especially a religion whose moral demands are so palpably out of reach—be born again, be perfect, be as a little child—must contain an answer to the question, *How is their fulfillment possible?* Its essence will be found in the answer to this question and not in the code only.

The answer cannot be found in the idea of duty: it must lie in a disclosure of the nature of the world. For a demand upon feeling calls for a transformation of desire; and desire, formed in us by nature, can be transformed only by a vision of unsuspected beauty and meaning in the heart of things. If man can somehow fall in love with the Real, as source of life, he may fall out of love with his self-absorbed self; and it is hard to see how else he can be "reborn" in the orientation of his affections.

In other words, rebirth, not being something a person can *do*—hence an impossible object of command—is not impossible as an experience. But it must come to a person as all values come—through discovery, through an encounter with some character in things that elicits spontaneous allegiance. The issue is the same today as in ancient times, though the language is different. Contemporary psychiatry, occupied in its own way with changing motivation, speaks of a need for "integration," will-focusing, and asks in effect how integration can be achieved. John Dewey offers an answer. In his notable essay, *A Common Faith,* he avers with great candor that the human person cannot integrate himself: he must find in his environment an activity that sustains and unifies his ideal ends. These our ideal ends have their own intrinsic authority; but they must not be "rootless ideals, fantasies, utopias": there must be in the universe natural conditions that promote "an active relation between ideal and actual."[17]

Taking the world at its surface value, it is quite possible not to find any such will-moving character. The comment "I find much in the world to call out my curiosity, even my wonder, nothing that calls out my reverence" easily finds echo. It is to this impoverished world sense that Christianity has spoken. In presence of the Roman lostness, convinced chiefly by power, it has represented the ultimate power as an active love—not a distant cosmic benevolence, but an aggressive will, seeking more than the confidence, the response of each individual soul. Most improbable! Yet in that response lay the moment of the demanded rebirth, the condition of the peace of each such soul: it alone could be his "salvation." [18]

[17] *A Common Faith*, 18 ff., 51. Have we not here an honorable lapse into metaphysics?

[18] In agreement with this need for an outer Real, which makes of religion something more than the dutiful service of moral ideals as abstract universals, Royce places the "Problem of Christianity" in the relation of each person to a Community, whose spirit is the interpreter of his moral experience. This experience is one of loyalty and disloyalty, of isolation, alienation, despair, of redemption through vicarious suffering of the atoning and interpreting spirit. No one, I think, has more deeply understood the passion of the early church, and its permanent meaning for humanity. No one has so wisely lifted the Pauline legalisms to the level of the dialectic of a loyalty inseparable from love. In Royce's thought, the Christian virtues take their due place as universals of the moral life of man. Their meaning and fulfillment would seem to depend on the actual existence of such a Community. Royce's discussion leaves open the question whether his Interpreter has historic identity or whether it remains in the realm of an ideal society like the brotherhood of all true Stoics. Its ideality doubtless remains purer and its reach more unlimited if it be an object of faith rather than of sight; the historic soon ceases to be immaculate. But in that case, the figure of Jesus, the prime mover, retreats behind that of Paul, the architect of the community's moral hierarchy. In my view, Christianity is committed to the radical step into the historic particular as the completion of its concept of incarnation as an actualized ideal. Otherwise it is not literally true

The essence of the Christian world view is this most unlikely doctrine about the nature of Being, that the most Real is the all-loving. If through his own perception one discovers this to be the case, the essence of the Christian code becomes possible, even imperative—namely, that desire itself be changed—that self and world be "overcome" through a love that suffers in order to create, seeing the neighbor now as what he is—not only, with Kant, as a free being, hence requiring respect; and not alone as an object of divine regard, hence calling out love and service; but also as himself having something of the divine in him— "ye have done it unto me"—hence worthy of reverence, "even the least of these." This the deepest reach of the Christian ethic is an immediate consequence of the deepest reach of its world view, whereby each person participates in the life of God.

The world view and the code are inseparable.

Two aspects of this view call for special comment, the place of suffering and the meaning of "perception."

As to the place of suffering:

While there is no Christianity without the acceptance of suffering, as implied by the symbol of the Cross, Christianity is not primarily sacrifice—it is power through sacrifice. The goal is not defeat of the human will, but victory of the transformed will. The ethic of Christianity cannot be read in literal applications of the Sermon on the Mount in its clear-cut contrasts with what "hath been said by them of old time"—in deliberate "hard sayings," hyperbole in the field of behavior used in order to compel attention to the realities of motive, e.g., if thy right hand

---

that the ideal is in the actual, and is the ultimate power of the history in which were immersed. See below pp. 119–24.

offend thee cut it off; take no thought for the morrow. On their face these are not "counsels of perfection"; they are counsels of immorality. The ethic of Christianity is not altruism nor mere pacifism nor drifting-in-idleness. It is superiority to the efficiently trivial, the reputably prudent, and the timorously pious. It is the prophetic conscious-ness [19]—a command of events through hard-won identity with the deeper realities, the eternal conditions of eternal good. The goal is the ineffable joy of one who has created something immortal because the quality of integrity is in it. Its life is the spur of co-operation with the absolute, at whatever pain and through whatever opposition. This is finding and doing one's task as the will of God; it is the working version of "Thy Kingdom come"; it is also love to one's neighbor. For, as Nietzsche has truly said, in one of his unconscious tangencies with Christianity, "Great love is, the beloved to create; and all creators are hard," first of all to themselves. To Jesus of Nazareth, his Way was one, not of acquiescence, but of sternly decisive oppo-sition to the hypocrites and the money-changers: it was a *will to create through suffering*. That will is the essence of the Christian ethic.

As to the meaning of "perception":
I have said that the Christian ethic implies a "most un-likely world view"—unlike what we perceive. With every religion, but more explicitly than most, it makes appeal to "faith"; and faith at once suggests a confidence in some-thing *not* perceived, a repudiation of what common-sense empiricism would report of the facts—passing, confused, and recklessly unjust. To a serious and conscientious real-ism, there may be something not alone softly optimistic

[19] *The Meaning of God*, ch. XXXII, 501 ff.

but downright unscrupulous in believing good of such an obviously mixed world.

Faith is indeed often a rejection of what appears indubitable—"the real world cannot be so cruel and so futile as this"—a postulate, not a perception. It is characteristically directed to another and better world, a world of supernature, heaven, whose character cannot be inferred from any laws of nature—this nature. Yet I am asserting the further paradox that faith, however far it reaches, cannot hold itself apart from either natural reason or natural experience; and yet that at its source it is a mode of perception. I affirm that what we have a right to believe of the *real depends on what we can see* of its inner nature.

Let me point out first that no one lives without suffering, nor without the faith that carries that suffering. The "will to create through suffering" is not the will of the exceptional, the heroic, the saintly: it is the will present in the labor of man and in the travail of woman. The faith that supports these sufferings and turns the two curses of Genesis into the pride of the race is simply the unbreakable thong of connection between the remonstrating tissues and the sense of the goal as the glory of the human lot. Something is borne because something is being born. Nature and history, not known but felt, hold silent fellowship with these passages of anguish, and the sufferer aware of their presence cannot doubt the meaning of his pain. There is something elemental, call it the *élan vital*, that faces every new experience with the impetus of past generations, carrying with it the original substance of things hoped for: it lives by faith. And this faith is less a theory than a perception.

Faith as a tension against appearances can be defined as a reversed skepticism, a refusal to be taken in by the first look of experience. In this sense faith is a natural ally of all thought, an ingredient of thought, as science pursues its adventure far beyond the borders of the imaginable. The *deus absconditus*, the concealed absolute, of the scientist lies indeed in a different direction from that of the soul seeking the moral realities—they are asking different questions. But they are alike concerned with power—always invisible—the one with power in nature, the soul with the ultimate power. It is a part of ancient wisdom that the ultimate powers are averse to display—the most powerful the least self-assertive. In the Hebrew prophets and in the greater mystics, the Almighty is in the still, small voice, or in the nonaction of Tao. If Christianity develops this theme symbolically in the weakness of the divine babe, the humility of the carpenter, the poverty and homelessness of the man of sorrows, the public disgrace of the condemned, forsaken and crucified, laying in futility itself the foundation of an invincible kingdom, it is but giving narrative embodiment to an insight with which in principle neither ancient wisdom nor the latest science has any quarrel. Christianity presents its narrative as *the clue* to the world riddle, and as such, an object of faith.

But the faith which Christian ethic requires is something more than a faith in a principle. It is this, but it is also—if you will permit the word—a *faith in fact*; that is to say, in the particular and present drive of experience. The faith of the pioneer settler, of the artisan at his labor, of the artist at his easel, of the woman in childbirth, yes, of the child also in his will to "grow up," is not faith in a generality. It is an immediate perception of, and commit-

ment to, *the forward thrust of being,* in this particular
present world of hidden powers, felt but inarticulate. This
never-assertive but never-absent metaphysical sense of
process-and-direction to which all action trusts itself is, I
dare say, the most primitive form of faith object; and our
commitment thereto the dimmest version of natural religion. But it may point to the one matter that now concerns
us, that religion is always in the last analysis autobio-
graphical: "This one thing I know." And my proposal is
that until one thus knows by *seeing* he has neither the
right nor the power to "believe."

The good faith of a religion will then appear in its
appeal to experience, first that of its prophet as an example of his own teaching, then that of each believer. For
Christianity this means that God's work and love are perceivable by each human being—not as past history—but
in his own way and context and time. "Behold, I stand at
the door, and knock: if any man hear my voice, and open
the door, I will come in to him, and will sup with him, and
he with me." The "any man" is significant. To make these
two words good, the being who speaks them—here called
"the Spirit"—must be, as the man of Nazareth could not
be, omnipresent in space and time—as it were *an unbound
and unlimited Christ,* pervasive of the world and of history, like the Logos of John's Gospel who "was in the
beginning with God," and at the same time universally
accessible—more than that, universally *initiative* of the
personal relation. The scope of this great saying, to my
mind the most impressive coming out of the experience of
the early church, enlarges as we dwell on it: it is unexam-
pled in its union of unlimited sweep with its complete self-
giving to each individual soul, however circumstanced.
The concept of the Christ involves the idea of a mediator

between man and God, an idea which historic mysticism has often been disposed to reject on the ground that each individual must find his own way to God in immediate experience. But every religion, including every variant of mysticism, is a *way* to this immediacy: reaching the non-mediated is a passage beyond mediation, *by aid of* that mediation. A purely immediate experience would be empty of meaning: our most nearly immediate experience, self-awareness, is mediated by the current rill of sensation and the contents of memory and purpose. To find God in immediate experience, which is indeed the substance of religion as experience, is therefore to find him through some mediation. If "the heavens declare the glory of God," it is nature that here serves as mediator. The concept of the Christ is the concept of a personal being whose presence "declares the glory of God" with the more adequate immediacy of companionship: "I will come in to him and sup with him, and he with me." If the author of the Johannine Epistles is right, love itself is a mediator: "Every one that loveth is born of God," and genuine love bears out this radical assertion. The Christ concept has its legitimate concentration; but also its legitimate release, important for the age to come, and in this passage strikingly made a part, though a neglected part, of Christian teaching.

Through these words, the Christian concept of religion recognizes that the lone ego in its exigency requires, not solely the truths of a philosophical generality, and not only a historical example of its code realized in an authentic life, but also each man's personal discovery that the ostensibly indifferent world conceals, as its reality, an intimate and individual concern for that ego, as of parent for child. This discovery can only be a person-by-person event, since it is the irreducible I-am that has to confirm the presence of an actual Thou-art, at the nucleus of its experience. It is there.[20]

Such an experience of personal discovery would be a sufficient answer to the hostile or secret-hiding appearances whether of fortune's brute fact, or of the scientific night view, or of the now opening astrophysical vistas that tend to bury beneath unthinkable immensities all significance of mankind and of man's eccentric planet. These judgments of vanishing worth are the illusions of a fallacious empiricism, valid in its field but partial and unseeing. The personal answer—the mystic's answer—is the genuine empiricism, to those who find it, sufficient and unlosable, and at the same time in its nature valid for all.

For the "mystic" here is simply that "any man" in any religion who opens the door of his self-built enclosure, and sees the world, perhaps for the first time, in his own experience, as not his alone but God's world, and therewith every

---

[20] This extraordinary sonnet, "Light of Men," published only after Charles Rann Kennedy's death, brings into juxtaposition—almost into union—three factors of motivation: one's own effort toward perfection; the demand of perfection as an outer "agonist" struggling with the self; the Logos of John's Gospel as an unbound Christ:

Ill-furnished though I am, I yet insist
Upon perfection, something which I see
Coming my way distinctly, meant for me,
My sole salvation gleaming through the mist.
Behold Him yonder, the dread agonist
That ever strives with me: yea, knee to knee
Breast against breast one heartbeat, vis-a-vis,
Flaming with joy of battle, keeping tryst!
He is the light that burns in every man
That comes into the world! He is the gleam
Of God that first awakens us, the dream
That glorifies our deeds, perfection's plan
Made plain, the Lord and archetype supreme
Behind all life since ever life began!

(From *World Within*: a Cycle of Sonnets, by Charles Rann Kennedy, edited by Margaret M. Gage, 1956, p. 62. Used by permission of Margaret M. Gage).

man's world, as held in God's care, the ego's personal
entity included. Such seeing is not a rare and privileged
event; it is not unnatural; it is a passing from the unnatural to the natural and true. It is present in some
degree in every wakening of the mind to love, and every
opening of the eyes to beauty: no one is so poor as not to
have felt *their* light and their liberation—even though it
be true that "most forget." "Love wakes men once a life-
time each," said Coventry Patmore; and the fact of having
seen is indelible.

To *hold to the meaning of this disclosure* of the Real is
the work of faith. And with that faith, and the reborn love
of life it brings, the will to create through suffering raises
its head. The world view of Christianity and its code, as we
have said, are inseparable.

Faith, natural and Christian; nature and supernature.
As the nucleus of a world view, the simple perception of
which we have been speaking seems far from the elaborate
traditional outlook of the church. The early church
Fathers seldom appealed to it in their formulations of the
creed. In the original teaching of Jesus, however, it often
came to evidence: he was keenly aware of the continuity
between the faith he repeatedly called for and the vital
faith of the living creation. His frequent appeals to his
followers—"O, ye of little faith"—to "consider the
ravens," or even the lilies of the field, are calling attention
to this natural *élan*. And far more universally, the "daily
bread" of the Lord's Prayer surely refers to *sustainment*
in the full gamut of its meaning—the totality of those
conditions, physical, social, cosmic, uncontrollable by our
own prudence, to which our action trusts as we throw ourselves forward upon an invisible future. There will be

harvest, the stars and the seasons, and human nature about us, and the quest of the unknown, and out of the unknown —succor. If Santayana chooses to call this natural trust "animal faith" his words are accurate—for the animals— and valuable, as registering the continuity between animals and man, even in this matter of faith; but there is in man *no line* at the animal level. Man's vital faith has the distinctive character of all human mentality; namely, that a sense of the whole is present in every part.[21] And for the "average man," perhaps for everyone, this sense of the whole is one of movement-with-direction; there is change everywhere, but not aimless change. Given the intersubjective factor—always present, if our analysis of experience is valid—the human whole sense will have the quality of purposiveness, movement toward a goal—*telos* as we have called it. The "animal faith" of man is thus the outgoing of man's life process toward a corresponding life process in outer reality, which outgoing we might call the unceasing prayer of being alive as men.

Faith is natural as breathing. I have referred to John Dewey's appeal for a common faith in an objective source and support of our "ideal ends," for which objective support he was willing, under strict limitations, to use the term "God." There are, he asserts, "natural forces and conditions that promote" the unity of our ideal will-aims and aid their realization. His emphasis is on the word "natural"; his enemy, the "supernatural." [22] In my view the ground of faith is indeed natural—here I agree with Dewey and with Max Otto; [23] and I insist with them on the continuity between "natural piety" as piety toward nature

---

[21] *Preface to Philosophy*, 16.
[22] *Op. cit.*, 51.
[23] See Appendix.

and whatever is honestly "mystical" in man's spontaneous reverence toward the world. But the opposition between the natural and the supernatural needs a second look.

The line between nature and supernature is a boundary for a specific purpose—that of science. And further, it is a natural boundary! The term "nature," like the term "self," has, as we might put it, a *double boundary*: in the narrower sense it excludes its negative, the nonnatural or the nonself; in the wider sense, each includes its negative. It is the human being, in the natural use of his reason, who defines what he means by "nature"—leaving himself, the definer and purposer, out of the scope of the "nature" he defines, at the moment of that definition: he defines a realm of natural necessity, of what used to be called "causes"; but he, the definer of that realm, is not caused by anything in that realm to do the defining. He remains free and purposive, while setting up his "closed group" of law-ruled events. In a strict sense, he in that act is "super"-natural; and all that is free, purposive, and creative in the universe belongs with him to a supernature, natural in the wider sense. Thus faith, which is natural, is also faith in a supernatural.

This nuclear perception, the central tie of individual man to his total environing world in its felt moral unity, is certainly not the whole of faith. But it is the germ from which all wider faith grows. Given the responsive outreaching of the inescapable I-am toward the equally inescapable (and naturally supernatural) Thou-art, animally instinctive if you or Santayana like, freedom and duty become items of your faith; also the certitude that your peace has its moral conditions in your use of that freedom —the item of "sin" appears in your world sense whether or not the word enters your creed. And as the simplest faith is the charter for action, and all action invades the future, faith must present a structural scheme of all futurity, claiming that futurity must provide a possibility of non-futility for human life; and hence that death itself, unquestionable encounter, must be a relative, not absolute, consummation of being in nothingness. For if the Something that I am has its conclusion and summation in Nothing, then faith is from the beginning a deceit. Natural faith extends to the relativity of death.[24]

The deep naturalness of Christianity grows on me as I write. Even in respect to the "sense of sin" which has given so many themes to theological punitive zeal and the fears of the sick soul from St. Paul to Calvin and the Puritan shores of America.

To much of the modern spirit, and indeed to the robust self-confidence of normal humanity, Christianity has seemed, and seems, unnaturally preoccupied with the ideas of sin. And I would stand with the firm human sense of right in the cosmos, ready to call God to account as well as to be called to account: whoever and whatever is responsible for my existence must respond to my just demand that existence-as-aspiring-being shall not be a condemnation to futility. This postulate of right, as I have maintained for many years, even in the form of resentment against apparent frustration, is one of the perennial sources of the idea of God.[25] This clearly seen, we must then note that the idea of sin is not an arbitrary insertion into developing religion, but a necessary consequence of man's occupation with an absolute ideal—or, as we have

[24] A theme to which I shall return in the volume on *Death and Life*.
[25] *Meaning of God*, 145 f. *et passim*.

put the matter, with requirements of the impossible, such
as the call for perfection.

The sense of sin is, in the first instance, simply the
shadow of uncompromising standards. But *whose* standards? We lose half of the fact if we impute them to the
"will of God," and three-quarters of the fact if we fancy
them as "Platonic Ideas" floating eternally in a tran-
scendent ether. They are demands which the soul of man is
bound to hold over itself. (For who could say, for example,
"I decline to accept the standard of perfection; my standard is three-quarters of perfection"?) The situation is, as
Reinhold Niebuhr so clearly recognizes, that the absolute
ideal "grows up spontaneously in human nature." [26] Judgment by this ideal is inescapable, not because it is God's
judgment, but because it is at the same time man's own
judgment of himself. It is man's glory that he can know
and apply this absolute standard: it is a part of his *participation in God's nature*. It is the prerogative of man's
type of knowing—and we have seen modernity perplexed
by its own inability to resign this prerogative in presence
of its advance in subjectivity—the prerogative of *knowing the universal*, which compels him to know his defect
as it is, and not as a flatterer would ease it. It is his mature
strength that he can justly and unflinchingly estimate his
own weakness.

Hence Vivekananda was mistaken when he said, "It is a
sin to call men sinners." He was right when he said that
men are offshoots of God: it is precisely because of the
God-nature within them that they—not we others—*call
themselves sinners*. It is an artist's suffering that he cannot
bring to his canvas the eternal meaning in what his eyes

[26] *The Self and the Dramas of History*, 141.

are fixed upon. But he would be the last to propose either that that beauty should be defaced to meet his powers, or that he himself should be deprived of the tormenting joy of absorbing-through-presence what so far eludes his grasp.

It is through its dwelling on sin that Christianity for the first time does full honor to human nature.[27] It does not dwell thereon in despair!

Christianity as deed: essence requires existence. The natural faith in what is beyond me is essentially a faith in kinship; man's trust in the real, as soul of the whole, is trust in the connaturalness of being, both as source of support and as source of demand. Religion has always inclined to represent this kinship in the guise of pananimism: Christianity represents it in the guise of the Fatherhood of God, perceived in experience.

As personal experience, crucial item of autobiography, such a perception-born faith might remain a private illumination and nothing more. But if private experience

[27] Hence, while accepting the principle of Omar Khayyám's bold reversal of court: "For all the sin wherewith the face of man is blackened, man's forgiveness give—and take"! we must suspect the thoroughgoing self-absolution thus invited. There is, however, one touch of sin which I regard as a merit, and for whose acceptance I would invoke neither Omar nor yet Reinhold Niebuhr, but rather the conscience of the artist who, at some point, *must call his work done*! He knows its imperfection; yet he knows, too, that he cannot forever rectify. The price of his bearing *any* fruit is that he retains the capacity to reject the importunity of the absolute, which would reduce him to barrenness and despair. This "calling done" what is not done—and the same is true of every work that embodies an infinite goal, finishing a book, for example—contains an ingredient of sin, of presumption. Yet if in the work the worship of the perfect has been genuine, the piece called done will witness beyond itself to what was aimed at: and where this is true, perhaps the forgiveness is conveyed together with the sin. I surmise that all fertility may contain this moral cost, and moral repair.

is—as we may now assert with good conscience—experience of the universal, it will press for transmission. In its own nature, our most primitive human illumination is a breaking out of solitude into a possessed intersubjectivity, which is also consubjectivity. Through the love born in it as a response, the discovering and realizing self is under inner pressure to spread its light.

And its first task as faith-spreading will be a summons to others *to see*—not as accepting general propositions about the cosmos, though the time for such truths will come, but as *seeing*. And presumably as seeing in the same human context in which the soul was first awakened. For the lover, bound to convey universal truth to its rightful receivers, can hardly fail to dilate on the merits of the particular other in whom he has caught his vision of the Absolute. That other, for him, is "the Way."

Thus the meaning of individual experience tends to unfold in a continuing community of witness bearers, at once a product of individual rebirth and a source of further rebirths. Through its self-propagating impulse, the inherent universality of its perception will tend to make itself actual in the structure of history (*The Meaning of God*, ch. xxxiii). The prophetic deed of the original Teacher, his self-commitment to a course involving his death as a factor in laying the foundations of "a Kingdom of Righteousness," thus becomes not merely an item of history long left behind, but a moving front *contemporary to all subsequent times*. Religion can call for no faith in what was, except as a faith in what is.[28]

[28] Cf. Kierkegaard: "There is no disciple at second hand. . . . For whoever has what he has from God himself clearly has it at first hand; and he who does not have it from God himself is not a disciple." *Philosophical Fragments*, 88, 84.

Now the prophecy of the prophet, that from his own deed and sacrifice will proceed an always contemporary and ultimately universal persuasive force actualizing in human history a reign of truth—this prophecy may conceivably fail. But the truth it embodies, the essence of the Christian world view, that God loves the world—this world —and works there to bring it to himself, asserts a will that cannot fail. For God cannot fail. This truth, then, is not valid as pure truth: it is not valid unless it makes itself good. For the Christian to give the world up as lost is to give God up, and to reject the validity of his vision.

It belongs therefore to the essence of Christianity that its world view is being actualized in history. It may be a misuse of language to say that for Christianity existence is an essence; but it is accurate to say that *it is essential for Christianity that its essence exist.*

We thus complete our answer to the question as to what Christianity is. Its essence is threefold, creed, code, and deed—a code and a deed, rooted in a faith, which in turn springs from a personal experience, a perception of the nature of things.

The faith: That the nature of things is divine love for the created world, a love that suffers;

The code: That desire must be reborn as active love, a will to create through suffering;

The deed: The movement initiated by such a will, as creating the conditions for the nonfutility of all such wills. Thus the kingdom is being actualized, a slow leaven in human history, or in another figure, a war of persuasion in a world of free wills.

v. *Is Christianity as a Whole Universal?*

WE ARE now prepared to deal with the question, To what extent is Christianity universal, or may it become so? That it has universal elements will not be doubted. But as embedding these universals within a detailed and history-marked corpus of faith, is it still in nature Hebraic, Greek, Roman, Western?

As to its essences of precept and doctrine—they do at least rise beyond all provincialism. And whether in spite of their defiance of possibility and probability, or because of it, they move toward world validation.

The Prophet of Nazareth was indeed careful to declare his teaching as the fulfillment of the Jewish Law: his inductions were the essence of that specific tradition, and of no other—they might well remain qualified by that fact. But it was his offense in the eyes of his own religious authorities that his teaching broke away from its own local orthodoxy. The questions his inductions answered were indeed the questionings of thoughtful Jews, but they were also the questionings of the Empire and of mankind. On this account, his answers could spread as they did, "to the Jew first, and also to the Gentile."

It lies in the nature of all induction that it shakes off the limitations of its actual collection of data. Its genius is that a few instances may represent the whole; its most daring achievement, that *one instance* may represent the whole! [29] And while the current theory of induction inclines to make a vast boast of humility, as aiming at noth-

[29] Aristotle, *Posterior Analytics*, 71 & 8: "Induction exhibiting the universal implicit in the clearly known particular." See also 100: "When one of a number . . . has made a stand, the earliest universal is present in the soul."

ing and yielding nothing but probable hypothesis, it may, as I have suggested, light on truth universal and necessary. Indeed, if there is any such truth, a gifted inducer might have hard work to avoid lighting on it as "his hypothesis." Newton hit upon the law of inverse squares empirically, but with a strong suspicion, later confirmed, that in the nature of physical things within his premises it had to be that way! In the field of morals, such an induction, rebuking natural impulse as a deeper nature in oneself rebukes it, would touch the minds of hearers with an appeal proportionate to its radical demand—perhaps with an odd sense of Platonic reminiscence, as of a haunting consideration long familiar to the subconscious self. Its discovery and formulation would be dated events, but they would appear as dated *releases of the eternal* [30]—and while subject to restatement, would enter the store of the "unlosables."

The Christian essences of precept belong to this store. Announced authoritatively and unargued, they either convince without argument or are dismissed as preposterous. And as having a certain finality through their inductive power, they are capable of interpreting other inductions, converging but less powerful, over a wide range of the religious experience of mankind.

Their finality is not inconsistent with the need of restatement and must be understood with that condition. No universal stands alone: each must confirm its validity through holding its place in the total and growing body of truth. Human thought has an unremitting duty to integrate and reintegrate this mounting store. Every con-

---

[30] I say "releases" rather than "revelations," for there is no revelation receivable that is not at the same time a release of the inner light.

tinuing truth becomes related to new items of knowledge, and every such new relation is a new judgment. Because of this, it is easy to adopt the *non sequitur* that no truth is permanent. One might as well say that because each addition to the family alters the parents, the parental identity is lost. It is precisely because of this constant reassembling that the factors of permanence become salient as structural elements of the growing totality, elements whose identity marks the identity of the whole.

Christian teaching in its origin asserted finality, but in a language that purposely left room for growth. Much of it wore a deliberately cryptic manner, as only for those who, "having ears to hear," possessed the key. The intentional nonliterality of many sayings—their practical absurdity if literally taken—was an effective way of *putting first things first*: "Therefore take no thought, saying, What shall we eat? or, What shall we drink? or, Wherewithal shall we be clothed? . . . But seek ye first the kingdom of God." And if the Teacher was right in his identification of the first things, no amount of reordering among the secondary things can disturb this status: what was thus placed first remains first.

Two thousand years have seen immense shifts in the furniture of the good life and also of the right life. They have opened questions in politics and economics, and in the picture of social evolution, that lay far beyond the horizon of that time. The normal roles of the primary instincts, including pugnacity, sex love, and acquisition, the importance of responsible self-care, ambition, foresight, enterprise, competition—mastery of nature, accumulation of knowledge—have become recognized elements of morality. The early Christian *contemptus mundi*, suiting itself perhaps instinctively in a crumbling empire to a conserving role of cultural reversion-to-the-chrysalis, over-weighted its message on the world-rejecting side. The Renaissance was in order not alone for a more courageous humanism, but for a truer Christianity as well. And modernity realizes that competition, with its factor of self-esteem, self-confidence, self-assertion—while subordinate, as in sportsmanship, to a just regard for the integrity of the "game"—cannot be eliminated from any community valuing its own health. Yet "seek ye first" remains unaltered and unalterable. And the hammer blows of the Teacher against greed, lechery, vindictive rancor, cowardice in serving truth, his radical revolt against ease in moral mediocrity—the "adjusted" life—retain their tonic pertinence, partly because of their linguistic intemperance, seldom seriously misunderstood. The essences of precept we have considered stand as true universals, independent of their historical origins. They convince as ideals even when the rankling problem of practical validity remains unsolved for lack of the presupposed world view.

World view, theology, and revelation. Now if the validity of the Christian essence of precept depends on the validity of the Christian world view, our intuitive assent to the spirit of the precepts carries with it a presumption of the validity of its premiss—the appeal of the ethic lends support to the metaphysic. But the cases are somewhat different: the world view as the crucial factor requires separate consideration.

Since the substance of the Christian faith is given in a perception available to "any man" in his own context and time, an element of universality is, as we observed, built into its nature. But it is a contingent universality—"If any man hear my voice, and will open the door. . . ." This

appears at first to put the Christian world view on a par
with the universality of empirical science, whose findings
are in principle verifiable by all observers. But it is on a
different footing in two respects. First, its truth cannot be
confirmed by all observers, because it cannot be confirmed
by *any* "observer": the conditions for confirming are not
dispassionate, they are moral and personal.[31] And at the
same time, it cannot be received as scientific truth has for
the most part to be received, solely on authority, i.e., as a
valid generality established by the experiment of author-
ized others. Rather, it must be received by each one
through his own experience. The Christian world view is
willing to achieve actual universality only through the
absolute particularity of its address, to each one severally.
This is its point of honor.

Because of this personal condition, it might be inferred
that there will always be a line of division in the world
between those who *see* and those who do not see. What to
some is universal truth, will to the others be universal
falsehood, based on wishful thinking. In a sense, this division is the actual situation. But if I am right, the faith of
the Christian is continuous with the nature faith by which
all men live—the light that, at least dimly, "lighteth every
man that cometh into the world." It is the *making-fully-
explicit of this universal faith.* It is therefore present in
some degree wherever religion is present. And religion is
so far natural that its basic faith—always coexisting with
the natural obstacles to faith—can be excluded only by a
definite act of rejection, as by force of an inconsistent
theory—a night view, perhaps—held with conscientious

---

[31] Pure objectivity, as keeping one's self out of the picture, destroys
the basis of the experience. This is largely the theme of Gabriel Marcel's
penetrating *Journal Métaphysique.*

resolution, waiting theoretical release. Christianity must acquire in its equipment theoretical answers to acquired theoretical embolisms of this sort. In substance, it has only to remove obstacles, not to insert an alien content, since, as Tertullian saw, "the human mind is naturally Christian." It may speak everywhere for its own essence-of-faith with confidence in its universality, as essence.

I say "as essence" because all theology outpasses the essence. Through a rightful alliance with imagination and art, and the just tendency of piety to multiply its objects of reverence, Christian theology like all others has admitted accumulations of detail tending to smother the stark simplicities of legitimate certitude. It has in times past developed a highly organized and pictorially specific other world, increasingly revolting to our intuition of the dignity of the ultimate mysteries of being. So far as this type of development is cherished and embedded in the corpus of required faith, universality is necessarily impeded. Nothing can be universal that offends this intuition, though the capacity of mankind, in presence of an indubitable jewel, to ignore its mounting is immense. This accumulation, therefore, has been and continues to be an object of reconception. The cause of universality does not demand that faith reduce itself to the bare minimum of natural piety; but it does demand that the area of dogmatic affirmation approach the simplicity of the essence, retaining the treasures of imaginative expression in the form of poetry, allegory, and symbol.

Note on revelation, reason, and repentance:
Theology has tended to protect the content of this accumulation by way of the concept of revelation—"Here God has spoken"; and the province of truth thus revealed has been held

to be precisely that which human experience and reason cannot reach.

If this line between provinces is absolute, dogma stands forever beyond critical judgment. But if truth is to be a unity —as it must be if human nature is to keep its own unity—the contents of revealed truth must have certification for our own minds: they must find place within the frame of what we continuously apprehend as "the whole." Any critique of pure reason must give good reasons for what lies beyond reason. If revelation is to be apprehended by faith, is faith, then, to be set in contrast with reason?

In speaking earlier of the basis of faith (above, p. 101), I have used the term "mystic experience," a term which like Bergson's "intuition" runs the risk of suggesting an esoteric or nonconceptual type of knowledge. I was careful to note that so far from being unnatural, "it is a passing from the unnatural to the natural and true." It is a wakening; and as such it may be abrupt and momentarily daze-begetting. One who having been on the wrong track suddenly regains his bearings is likely to be at first confused by the afterimage of his illusory sense of direction: his recovery may appear as an incursion from outside, perhaps as Saul-who-became-Paul was halted on the way to Damascus. But the vindication of his new perception is that it clearly recognizes the error: it takes the measure of both truth and falsehood, as if to say "Now for the first time I see things as they really are; hitherto, I have been blind." The appeal of the revelation is to one's own judgment —quite the reverse of setting that judgment aside by *force majeure*.

In the new light, the previous blindness is of course repudiated; and if that blindness is felt to be in some sense culpable, this repudiation is *ipso facto* a repentance. Faith in the new brings with it repentance of the old. Reinhold Niebuhr inclines, if I read him aright, to regard repentance a precondition of faith: he speaks (e.g. in *Faith and History*, 139) of "the repentance which is the presupposition of renewal of life." I suggest that the course of experience follows the reverse order: appealing from Niebuhr to Niebuhr, repentance is possible only when one sees that he was wrong, i.e., as the light dawns on him (*ibid.* 140, at bottom). Thus it is with the revelation involved in all love: *now one sees;* and as for one's previous condition which appeared to itself so rational, "Atheists are as dull who cannot guess God's presence out of sight"—the poet's analogy is exact. Repentance of that dullness is a consequence of the illumination: repentance is a consequence of faith (which is perception), not a precondition.

Given this change of order, it is no longer necessary to consider faith as something that supervenes upon the bankruptcy of human reason, or its entanglement in dilemmas with no apparent rational escape, in any other sense than that in which all empirical data come to us, as something given, not calculated in advance. Our great solutions arrive empirically; but they are none the less solutions. *Revelation is empiricism on the spiritual level.* It has the character of a solution, a fully rational character, not devised, but found. Faith is its recognition.

The deed and its history: problem of positive religion. But the essence of Christianity, if we are right, is not exhausted in precept and world view together. There is still the deed, and its history. A positive religion, which we have likened to a system of positive law, is a body of thought-and-precept entangled with a body of experience. That experience, personal and corporate, its history, becomes so far part of the being of a positive law system that such systems in Europe have not been interchangeable nor transferable from nation to nation in spite of a large common content of universal principle. Our chief problem lies here. Do the historical aspects of Christianity—which after all make up its personal identity—do they detract from or perhaps contradict the universality of the whole as a concrete movement?

Put the question the other way around. Is the religion of the world civilization to be "a" religion, or simply religion? Must it shed the particulars of founders, sacred books, acts of the apostles, councils, creeds, churches, sacraments, lives of the saints, commentaries and commentaries on commentaries? This is a plea that recurs; and to it John Dewey has given powerful support, voicing the temper of many a modern spirit long disaffected from contending details of organized religion, yet equally discontent with a religionless secularism. Dewey regards "A Common Faith" as a matter of urgency; but to reach it, he would "wipe the slate clean and start afresh . . . free from all historic encumbrances." [32]

This is not peculiarly a modern plea. In some degree it has characterized all the great reformers and founders, including Jesus of Nazareth. Is it perhaps an irony of history that each of the great universal religions, having dismissed one group of particulars, has taken on another; for each of them, having well distanced the localism of its background, has attached itself with even greater emphasis to the particular person of its founder. Is this, I ask, a bit of irony dogging every leap toward the universal, or is it an indirect evidence that religion, in its freest form, is not fully itself without identification as a continuing historic enterprise?

If this is true of any religion, it is true of Christianity with peculiar emphasis. For Christianity is explicitly the religion of "the prophetic consciousness"—that is to say of the affirmative relationship of faith to historic effect.[33] To Jesus, faith ought to be a power; and if it was not, there was something wrong with the faith. His was the original "satyagraha," spirit in control of fact, calling for power over events as a duty, and as an achievement if one have faith "as a grain of mustard seed." Less than any

[32] *A Common Faith*, 6, 8–11.
[33] *Meaning of God*, 518–24.

other religion, less than Buddhism or Islam, certainly
less than Hinduism, for the religion of Gandhi was half
Christian, can Christianity abstract its essential truth
from its historic being, the deed of its prophet, and the
doer.

Its particularity, however, is by no means limited to its
personal identification with the work and prophecy of its
founder; apart from this, it continues to carry a heavy
load of historical detail.

Its sacred books bear traces of its struggle with Greek
and Roman philosophies, and more than traces of its
Palestinian ancestry. It records, to be sure, its own breach
with the older teaching, and with the proprietary spirit of
Hebrew chosenness: if "God is able of these stones to raise
up children unto Abraham" the exclusive picture of linear
inheritance falls to the ground. But for this very reason,
the New Testament requires the Old Testament including
all the Hebrew history for its intelligibility. Christianity
was indeed a new beginning, and as a conscious effort to
subordinate all subsequent history to a universal idea, the
kingdom of God, its arrival marks a division point in the
flow of time. But it is a history-bound effort thus to subordinate history—otherwise it could mark no division
point!

What we here encounter is the irrational element in all
experience. The price of existence, of all decision and
action, is partnership with the irrational; if an idea is to be
more than idea, it must carry the accidents of time, place,
event context—factuality as it is found, nondeducible.
To "realize" an idea is to equip it with a here-and-now;
and every here-and-now has its irrelevant limitation. In
Christianity's early struggle for existence the irrational
element becomes a conscious issue: "to the Jews a stum-

bling block and to the Greeks foolishness." [34] As a philosophic teaching, it might have separated itself from these accidents. As a task, it could not do so, for its task was to make just these irrationals subserve the will of God—this *is* "incarnation."

Instead of shaking free from its particulars, Christianity accordingly inclines to preserve them as if they were precious elements of its universal gospel: it celebrates its own birthday; ritualizes the passion of its prophet; inclines to condense its message to mankind into two words, Follow Christ. As a movement it thus claims a personality of its own, as distinct, as odd, as steeped in peculiar, irrational circumstance as any individual personality.

Is its universality thereby compromised?

How can it fail to be?

Perhaps the best preliminary answer would be a particular answer, with the simple premiss that the "irrational"—strange to say—is what everybody understands: as empirical knowers, what we are most used to is the givenness of the given. Since all particulars are in a sense irrational, it would be irrational to expect existence without irrationality. The reception by any person—himself a reason wrapped in irrationals—of any new being, person, religion, will be governed by this understanding—not ignoring accidents of history and personality, *but unhindered by them.*

Let me illustrate by an instance from the Orient, where Christianity has been and continues to be under fire as exotic. I quote from a book by Yasaki Takagi published in Japan in 1954:

[34] Cf. A. A. Bowman's remarkable essay, *The Absurdity of Christianity*, 1931.

The fundamental weakness of the Meiji, that is, the modern Japanese civilization, was the mistaken notion that the various aspects of Western civilization—political, economic, and social —could be borrowed without adopting its spiritual foundation, and the failure to grasp the basic idea of individuality, which is to be traced essentially to Christianity. . . .

My personal conviction is that the Japanese are thus at a momentous juncture of their history, confronting the grave question whether they decide to engraft their own civilization into the tree of Western Civilization based on the Christian concept of human personality, which is after all, the major trunk of universal human civilization. This, it seems to me, is the only way to save our nation. . . .[35]

There is here a remarkably clear conception of civilization itself as an entity with an individual history, having all the extraneous attributes and the limitations of a groping and finite organism, and yet carrying universality in its arms.[36] What Dr. Takagi singles out of western civilization as needed by Japan is an "idea"—clearly a universal—"the basic idea of individuality . . . the Christian concept of human personality": why does he not suggest taking it *as an idea*, instead of as the sap of a concretely growing tree? Is it perhaps because rootage of an idea in the actual problems and confusions of strug-

[35] *Toward International Understanding*, 136 f.

[36] Professor Takagi's outlook, with its superiority to the *afterklang* of recent political passions, is not exceptional in his land. A slight incident may extend the picture. In April, 1955, I was inquiring of a Japanese in Washington about the present inclination of Japanese young people in religion. He reported that Buddhism and Shinto were declining in influence whereas Christianity was gaining: I was prepared for the first statement, but not for the second. I asked, "Do they then favor the religion of the recent enemy?" "No," was the answer; "They favor Christianity. But not as the religion of the enemy. As universal religion." The discernment of this answer is the more significant since it involves no repudiation of the historical *per se*. A recent writer, Dean Aikawa of Kanto Gakuin, Yokahama, puts the case even more sharply: "Young Japanese do not want to be loyal to the West any more; they want to be loyal to Christ." (*Christian Century*, Oct. 12, 1955.)

gling mankind, beside being a pledge of literal good faith, is *part of the meaning of the idea?*

If this is a fair clue to our dilemma, it may even be the case that the personality of a religion, as "steeped in irrational circumstance"—so far from compromising its universality—would contribute to its definition. Let us explore this clue.

We need take no issue with Plato as to whether every enfleshment of an idea involves some defacement of its perfect essence: we assume this probability. But I point out, as against both Plato and Kant, that existence, in the case of an idea of right living, is an element of perfection. For right living has to be realized in a limitless variety of circumstances, each one of which adds to the meaning of the load which "right living" has to carry: the experience of trying to carry out a precept is at the same time a thinking process reaching a judgment as to what that precept means. Any injunction to right feeling or action implies impediments thereto; the gift of free human creativity implies ever-new inventiveness, including inventiveness in ways of going wrong; the burden of the injunction, to be completely understood, will require a course of experience —let us say as long as the inventiveness of evil continues! Even as addressed to the single individual, whose exigency is always particular and unique, the meaning comes in full only with the embodiment in deed. The more comprehensive the induction of a precept, and the more unqualified its claim of finality through all time, the more indispensable is the wide-flung and long-lasting experience of applying it—it must have historic existence.

This requirement rests with peculiar emphasis on the command to love God and neighbor. Its summons is too easily spoken and accepted unless its meaning is charged with an infinite realism. Without a literal and continued encounter with circumstance, "love" is a generality unfit to carry the burden of religious faith in the age we now enter, forced as this age is to take the full measure of possible tragedy and also of the burgeoning potential cruelty of man's action on man. God's love to man must mean love on the part of *a being coinvolved in the existence of this world, such as it is.* To speak responsibly of this love, and of man's answering affirmation, religion must continually explore the expanding sense of its own finalities—it must be "a" religion, having its own experience.[37]

The assumption of my argument is that religion, and especially the Christian religion, is committed to the thesis that the will of God is to be done in this world.

There is indeed a sense in which all religion is a flight from the City of Destruction. The Christian's citizenship is explicitly elsewhere (a trait which led Rousseau to exclude him from membership in his ideal city-state); and the glory of his new life is that he "has overcome the world." Still, if he can achieve this overcoming, and reach a love of God or of life, only by an act of moral alienation from the grim detail of earthly affairs (as Berdyaev seems to propose), he has lost the secret of the vitality of this particular religion. For its vitality lies in the paradox

[37] It is just in this relation of experience to meaning—a position which I would *a priori* assume that a good pragmatist would favor—that John Dewey finds reason for seeking the jettison of specific historic religion, every "a" religion, whereas to me it calls for the concrete and explorative work of an identifiable religious community. The difficulty, of course, is in Dewey's objection to finality in any form, especially the finality of religious dogma, whereas in my view finality somewhere is the necessary condition of any intelligent experimentation. In the general necessity of experience to meaning, Dewey and I are in full accord.

whereby *detachment is a condition of more effective re-attachment*, an alternation well understood by the greater mystics, in which lies the germ of historical creativity, and its perpetual renewal.[38]

We cannot begin to understand the career of Christianity apart from its magnificent and radical ingredient of *contemptus mundi*, far more passion-filled than the Stoic's proud freedom-from-perturbation or the Buddhist's deliberate discipline of desire—and no doubt capable of fanatical excess.[39] But neither can it be understood without its equally magnificent adoption of this world and its history as locus of a cosmic drama, never to be abandoned to despair.

It is tempting to see religion in terms of but one phase of this strife of opposites. In a luminous essay, a recent commentator on *The Messianic Idea in Israel* points out that Judaism would never have affirmed that the kingdom of the Messiah "is not of this world." [40] For the Messianic idea, he holds, includes a definite political hope. And the Jewish Messiah is "a human being, flesh and blood, like all mortals." His kingdom is, in brief, a step toward the consummation of the meaning of human history, here and now.

This view is not in complete contrast with that of Christianity, nor of its founder. The man who (in the narrative, John 18) stood accused of calling himself a king, pleaded not guilty in one sense, but accepted the indictment in another. He declined to consider himself "king of the Jews"; he acknowledged headship of a kingdom of "truth." What he was repudiating in the words "not of this world" was

[38] *Meaning of God*, ch. XXVIII. *Thoughts on Death and Life* (1937), 178–204.

[39] See Friedrich Paulsen's marvelous chapter on contempt of the world in his *Ethics*.

[40] Joseph Klausner, as reviewed in *Christian Century*, June 15, 1955.

resort to the physical sword, as an instrument which, however useful in establishing power in this world, is wholly
irrelevant to establishing a kingdom of truth. He was definitely not rejecting the realm of this world as domain of
this truth, or of the Messiah's reign, or of God's kingdom.
His assertion of his own conquest of history stood intact:
"And I, if I be lifted up from the earth, will draw all men
unto me." Such drawing power, on the part of the prophet,
wholly inconsistent with the use of force or fraud, and
wholly independent of the political arm as of all political
prospect (whose inclusion would at once compromise its
spiritual integrity) must nevertheless be exerted here, in
this world, where "all men" are!

This drawing of men implies meeting their problems in
their own context, and continuing to do so as the context
changes. In general terms, the struggle of the Son of Man
with the adversities of his own life and his acceptance of
death are indeed typical of the human problem of faith in
all places and times; they need no supplement to symbolize
with complete literalness the fundamental precept of losing
one's life in order to save it. He doubtless regarded his
course toward death as so expressly an evidence and token
of his own conviction—the first human will-to-death on
precisely that issue, an issue which he himself had publicly
created—that no one thereafter, on that issue, could ever
be as he was—alone. As his followers would be confronted
by this same call to sacrifice, he would as pathbreaker be
with them, "even to the end of the world." And yet it was
part of his prospect to anticipate developments in their
experience for which further light would be needed: they
would wish to be "led into all truth." In their encounter
with emergencies whose shape only the endless devising of

the future would reveal, there would be the continuing disclosure of the purport of the unchanging identity of faith. Only an enduring historic continuity could fully reveal its meaning.

Significance of irrational; inescapable tension. We may now fairly affirm, in answer to the question raised above, that the history of a particular faith normally contributes to its definition; and that in so far as it does so, the universality of that faith is not compromised.

But it would be an error to infer from this that there is no tension between its historical development and its universal essence. We have two propositions to bear in mind. First, that a religion pertinent to human life, in order to be universal, must be particular—it must be a "concrete universal." Second, the particular aspects of such a historical movement are in *constant tension* with its universal character. This would be true were it only for the here-and-now limitation of a gospel emerging in human history, which seems from the outset to violate the necessary limitless reach of a Word of eternal import to all men.

This tension is perpetually renewed. The tendency toward enriching the content of faith, as experience reveals its implications, has to be constantly challenged by the demand for simplicity and identity with the original teaching. And the very process of self-discovery, applying the generalities of the precepts to changing conditions of life, the necessity of working in the given world in terms of current pressures, techniques, concepts—not to say with worldly methods—must come into clash with the demand for the original purity and unworldliness.

This clash was prompt to appear in Christian history. We find it full-fledged in the second century, as in the career of that stormy genius Tertullian, who after years of contest with churchly officialdom rejected his ardently espoused Catholicism for the crudely primitive and austere sect of Montanists. He felt a need to be near what had originally impelled him, a Roman, to the new cult—presumably the inner greatness of martyrs who "had something" which he and other well-placed worldlings had not.

Tertullian's unfinished struggle is still unfinished. It is pertinent to observe, in passing, that the mixture of the Christian essences with historical amalgam did certainly not prevent the spread of the faith in those early days. The broad historical fact that Christianity has been migratory indicates not only that its essences are not restricted in their appeal to special varieties of human nature, but also that its particulars have at least not fatally impeded their recognition—leaving open the possibility that they have helped it. It is true that these migrations have not been unattended by schism, attributable to some extent to this local variety: that Roman and Byzantine versions have pulled apart; that Nestorian Christianity, advancing through Asia even into China, went an independent way; that Coptic and Armenian Christianities, the ancient Christianity of southwest India, and various other semi-insulated Christian plantings, developed individual tenets and practices.[41] But it is also true, I believe, that while these variations have made their nests in the particular and pictorial phases of the faith, none of the variants has departed from what we have called the essence in its three-fold simplicity.

[41] Some of these deviations have been sufficiently wide to inspire the phenomenon of Christian missions to Christians—a matter which first came to my attention through the circumstance that a maternal aunt was for many years stationed at Mardin, Turkey, as missioner to Armenian Christians.

In this complex and diversified history, we are justified in limiting our attention for the moment to the European area, because it is in Europe that the Christian ethic and world view took firmest and for a time almost exclusive root, and it is also here that they have been subject to the most radical strains. It is these strains that are of decisive moment in judging the availability of Christianity for the coming civilization. Our present question then takes this form, whether the particularities of Christian history in Europe have beclouded its universality, or released it.

In this its western pilgrimage we may trace two broad phases—first from an original simplicity toward complexity, through extraordinary cultural creativity, with natural incidents of worldly entanglement and efflorescence of supernatural adornment; and then a reverse phase toward greater reticence, approaching simple identity with its essence. During its earlier periods, Christianity was *applying itself* with incredible energy, replacing a crumbling political order, molding institutions and arts to patterns it regarded as dictated by its world vision and ethos. Whatever our judgment of the result, the magnitude of this achievement constitutes a unique chapter in human history whose measure we are barely beginning to assess.[42]

In so doing it took the local coloring of the medium in which it was working: *it was in making "the West" that Christianity became "western."* Then, as we have seen,[43] it

[42] Beside several notable recent studies on the general topic of Christianity and Civilization, and Toynbee's monumental work, monographs on special aspects of cultural history have broken new ground, as in Roscoe Pound's notable lectures on religion and law. I cherish a dimming hope to be able to bring to print some part of a considerable MS. on "religion and civilization," sketched out during the past fifteen years.

[43] Above p. 82.

released these institutions and arts—not without struggle
—to discover their own independent groundwork. This
self-emptying inaugurated a new stage of self-discovery:
profiting by the free criticism of these its now secularized
offspring, it has been learning to identify itself with something less than Christendom as a whole. With what, then?
Has it shed its entire weight of cultural concreteness to
return to its original emptiness—the simple germinal essences inherently universal? If not, what is the goal toward
which this process points?

Double relationship to western institutions. Patently
the recent period, in which arts and institutions have gone
largely their own way, is one in which Christianity can no
longer accept responsibility for, still less identity with, the
resulting pattern of culture. It identifies itself today with
no institution (other than the ideal and unified church)
and with no set of institutions. Yet it holds itself pertinent
to all of them; it maintains the permanent attitude of responsible criticism. It is not, and never can be, an ideology,
specifying a program for world order with an economic
and political as well as moral goal; yet there is not a corner
of human life toward which it admits itself irrelevant.

With the disappearance of a Christendom which could
present itself as a model of applied Christianity, there has
emerged a *double relationship* to the institutional western
world which we must define with some care. There is a relation of freedom and a relation of involvement. There is
freedom from control and from carrying the sole burden of
creative and re-creative work. Christianity today is prepared to recognize its own germinal function in the *spirit*
of human relationships, rather than in their overt shapes,
none of which shapes can be declared deducible from the

spirit of love to God and neighbor. It would be false to say that Christianity is or has a "social gospel" in the sense that there is a specific form of property, polity, family, education, et cetera, deducible from the spirit of love. It would be equally false to say that there is no social gospel; there is a definite relation of involvement.

Let me illustrate. Christianity is certainly committed to "charity," whether in the broad meaning of *agape* or in the special meaning of aid to the needy. But whether this charity is to express itself in alms, or in aid to self-help with conserved self-respect, or in a frontal attack upon poverty itself, be it by general social reform or by economic revolution, deponent sayeth not. Christianity dictates no policy and joins no party; [44] yet it is applicable (sporadically or systematically) at any existing level of social intelligence. It assumes, probably rightly, that there will always be scope for charity: that the time will never come when one man can say to another, "I have no need to which you can minister," and when therefore the great saying "Inasmuch as ye have done it . . ." could have no application.

The fallacy of identifying any given form of property law with Christianity has become a commonplace. But to infer from this that Christianity is indifferent to the functions of institutions would be an even graver fallacy. Institutions as they stand are structures of a positive law whose draperies are circumstantial, but whose backbone seeks

[44] This has been well put by Gabriel Marcel in his recent book, *The Decline of Wisdom*: "The essential aim of knowledge and life is the ordering of oneself to the cosmos, rather than exercising a transforming action on a world which man might be regarded as having to subject to his desires or needs." This is wholly consistent with the aim of exercising a transforming action on human wills, and thus on human history, with consequent alleviation of misery—an essential phase, I take it, of the promotion of the kingdom of God in this present world.

absolute stability. If it can be maintained that the dignity of man, his freedom, and his development, require some form of property—yes, of private property as well as common property [45]—and if it is true that Christianity demands such freedom as an aspect of the soul's dignity, and has been the original protagonist of this requirement in the growth of western institutions, then we must say that there is *something within the law* of property for which Christianity stands, and will always stand.

Let us put the matter this way: in every social institution there are elements relative to the total internal balance of its particular society, and also elements of permanent validity. It is a current superstition that the relative, where it exists, excludes the absolute; the truth is that absolute and relative are commonly blended. And the presence of an absolute may be suspected even when its clean extraction long defies our efforts.

If this is the case with property, it is even more true of the family. There is such a thing as "the Christian family"; it has somthing to do with that same Christian reverence for individual souls and their freedom, the equal dignity of man, woman, child, the consequent call for adult choice in this the most momentous human alliance, and for a one-to-one partnership. It is perhaps not too much to say that the "Christian family" comes close to being an absolute, for Christianity a necessary consequence of its own universal precepts. For the family is the most direct embodiment of human love; and human love is, in its own complete self-consciousness, inseparable from the love of

[45] W. E. Hocking, "Problems of World Order," in *American Political Science Review*, Dec., 1952, 1121. See also "Private Property and Property Systems," in *Post War World*, 3, a publication of Federal Council of Churches, summarizing results of a subcommittee of the Cleveland Conference, Jan., 1945.

God. It is the natural context for a sacrament, inasmuch as it is by way of human love that the divine is most frequently and concretely discovered.

The spirit of human love carries the germ of its own law [46]—its disposition to exclusiveness, permanence, responsibility over the whole area of living, care of offspring (mindful of the chief joy of an earlier anthropology, that of discovering new variants of sex mores, I venture for brevity to be somewhat dogmatic about the natural trend of mature sensitiveness). The force of this intuition has made itself felt from the beginning, as the early church set itself against Roman practices of infanticide, the procuring of abortion, professional prostitution. And that in finding its own norm it has lighted on something universal may be indicated by the fact that in the Orient—here and there, with and without incitement from western sources—elements of adult freedom of choice in mating, of an ampler career for women, of monogamy, make their way, and tend—sometimes too swiftly—to dissolve the firm traditional groupings, as of the Chinese "great family."

At the same time, the relative is present with the universal. There is wide variation in family law among "Christian nations" in respect to rights of husband, wife, children. And the Christian principle of the dignity and worth of the individual soul speaks with uncertain voice when the marriage bond is no longer sustained by the spontaneous impulses of the partners. Laws canon or secular regarding divorce, remarriage, custody of children in cases of separation, appear to wander in the wilderness.

[46] I had a friend whose proof for the existence of God was "man, woman, and the moral law," implying that within the natural attraction there is an unvocal but invincible reference beyond the two selves directly involved to an overindividual requirement—ultimately to an absolute.

Institution of freedom from institutions. This freedom
of Christianity from whole commitment to social institutions may be regarded as itself an institution, and as such,
an institution whose position approaches that of an absolute. Though still misunderstood, particularly in America,
the degree of mutual independence which modernity has
achieved as between church and state must be reckoned
among its most important and durable accomplishments,
because by its aid individual freedom receives its most
pertinent setting. As the church has released its claim
upon, and so its responsibility for, the acts of the secular
state, the state *ipso facto* has released the church to define
its own province. But since that province is the revealing
to individual souls of the way to their own integration, the
state in freeing the church accepts the *freedom of individuals to define their own ultimate loyalties.* The central
motivation of each individual is thus placed beyond the
reach of the state, with the state's consent, and at the same
time beyond any but the persuasive power of the church.
What is genuinely universal in the field of will-aims is thus
enabled to rise before the mind to its due level at the time
and in the way suited to the life pilgrimage of each person.

Among all the fields of free action, this is the one of
absolute importance: it is the one unalienable element of
modern liberty; it is a right no institution can give nor
take away, but it is here institutionally protected from the
dominance of institutions.

And with this liberty is wrapped up whatever is universal in the principle of democracy and in the bills of
rights characteristic of modern constitutions. In their
specific forms, the actual democracies and the listed "rights
of man" include much that is not absolute. No religion
could endure the load of attempting to inject into the com-

ing world order, let us say, American democracy as a requirement of God's kingdom. But whatever is universal there—and it is present—can be found in its relation to the fundamental liberty and dignity of the person which Christianity can define.[47]

In sum, what we can clearly assert in regard to the institutional load which Christianity as particular religion has to carry is a twofold judgment. First, its modern experience has freed it from the sponsorship of any western institution as it stands. It is the perpetual critic of "Christion institutions"; its criterion of criticism is always the degree in which the institution in question fulfills the precept of love to God and neighbor, a precept of the spirit, from which no concrete institution can be deduced. Second, this precept does contain an affirmative social requirement. It carries corollaries as to elements of social structure—it creates as well as criticizes; only, its creative force has to associate itself with all other factors going to make up a positive national or continental culture. What it contributes tends to coincide with what can be recognized as absolute *within* a resultant clothed in relativity.

In any case, *the essence of the Christian precept is at the same time the essence of whatever social gospel Christianity may bear* into the world civilization before us. Christianity is thereby relieved of any burden of "westernism" its institutional associations may appear to impose, apart from its own central spirit. It is relieved logically, though psychologically it will doubtless be held guilty by association, until by the renewal of its creative vitality it

[47] It is the function of a philosophy freed from contemporary conformities to define the necessities in law and custom that underlie the purely positive. Cf. *Experiment in Education*, 158, 282–83; Jacques Maritain, *Humanisme Intégral*, chs. 5 and 6.

shows itself *capable of inspiring other institutional shapes* in altered historical contexts, embodying the same absolutes. It is all the more urgent that it realize at the present juncture its *identity with its simple essence,* visibly universal.

Note on the internal diversity of Christianity:
    To call for reconception in the direction of simplification, by identifying Christianity with its essence, raises the insistent problem of the pluralism and diversity of the Christian movement. It is especially during the modern period that Christianity has become multiform to an extent embarrassing to any discussion of its character which proceeds as if it *has* a single character. These internal differences, though in the end they may actually contribute to its clarity, do for the present tend to obscure it.
    The Protestant movement, in the interest of a freedom essential to the very concept of religion, has opened a gate to another freedom far more questionable—the freedom of anyone to identify what he personally sees, as the content of his own faith—to identify this with Christianity forthwith. I have insisted on *seeing* as the foundation of believing; I have assumed, however, a rigorous veracity in reporting what one sees. If the mystic is an honest reporter, what he reports will doubtless be a part of Christianity: it may not be the whole. The necessary liberty to declare and spread one's vision, interpreted as a liberty to establish a new sect of Christianity, has been so far magnified as to beget doubt in the pure observer as to whether there is an identical being rightfully claiming that name.
    My own feeling about the multiplicity of sects is that most of them that have become a factor in contemporary society have had some reason for existence: most "reforms" have been needed. But that the function of reform should be a function provided for *within the church,* not calling for schism, but for self-searching and reconception, in the persuasion that variety of expression which is not hostile to the essence may contribute to the life of the church. Differences become splits only if those

who hold the prior faith think that they have the whole truth —without excess and unimprovable. On this score, I am of the opinion that the variety is far in excess of what is necessary, inasmuch as very few variants of Christianity today would reject the simple essences here defined, and which are to this extent sufficient to unite them.

There is a sense in which Quakerism, whose genuine Christianity few will doubt, has best caught the genius of a particularity that is also universal. Quakerism is today giving powerful evidence of its universality, not only within but outside the Christian organizations, by exploring and finding common ground with mystical tendencies of Buddhism in Japan and of Hinduism in India. (Douglas Steere, "The Quaker Message," in *Christian Century*, Aug. 3, 1955.) If it tends to be in our time a common interpreter between religions, that is not to be taken as proof that validity in positive religion is dependent on minimality in organization and creedal elaboration, though it is clearly facilitated thereby. But it does suggest that the search for essence may still go far in the direction of simplicity without losing the substance of the matter. And in my view simplicity is still the great desideratum.

There is also a sense in which the conception of the church in its historic continuity, in its involvement with all the arts— an involvement not canceled by their liberation—and in its wide-flung responsibility for the souls of men, is best realized in the churches called Catholic.

I have known of a priest mounting a ladder set against the wall of a burning brick prison, to administer the sacrament to a prisoner doomed to die in the flames behind immovable iron bars—the priest being the only human being in that community to feel that concern and that responsibility. I have no inclination to subscribe to the special theological views which made that sacrament important. I have every respect for the spiritual community that could inspire that deed of danger, fellowship, and hope in the love of God.

Quaker and Catholic together bear their partials of a total truth, which includes the truth of a continuing historical community of aggressive *caritas* at once material and spiritual.

The Christian movement as a whole contains them both and much between them, without, as yet, a visible or conceptual synthesis. But not without a bond of meaning that can already be felt. In their coexistence, they constitute an enduring necessity for internal advance in self-understanding. And by that same sign, they exclude exclusiveness.

Is Christianity, then, as a whole, universal? My answer is that it is on the way to become universal, and that its travail through the western passes of modernity has qualified it, and requires it, to take a certain leadership in meeting the religious problems of the coming civilization. But further that this leadership can be held only by a humility, ready to acknowledge its own continuing need for reconception, in view of its present unfinishedness, and also of the depth and breadth of the religious experience of other lands. The moment calls for a heightened severity of self-consciousness on the part of all religion.

This labor of reconception is going forward. It is being aided at every point by the increasingly intimate encounters of Christianity with reanimated ancient religions in Asia and with the national tempers animated by those religions. Of the principles governing these encounters I have still to speak.

GUIDES OF INTERACTION AMONG UNIVERSAL RELIGIONS

i. *Affirmation Is not Exclusion*

THE intention of universality is not peculiar to any one religion. As our present century has justified the instinctive assumption of the human self that its thinking and valuing are the thinking and valuing of every man, so it justifies his equally instinctive assumption that his address-of-prayer is the address of every man. There is an inherent universality in the religious attitude itself that eternally counteracts the localism implied in the complementary necessity that religious observance and thought shall involve the whole man in his concrete social insertion. Every religion that reaches the degree of self-understanding fitting it for a career in the modernity inspired civilization we find gathering around us will know its own calling to universality. Less than ever is head-on clash a guide to truth and sanity, or to the discovery of a genuine religious goal for man.

* Portions of Study V appeared in *The Hibbert Journal,* July, 1956.

If, as I have held, faith is based on what a man sees, and not on what he merely supposes, Christian faith does not present itself as an hypothesis competing with other hypotheses: it exists at all only as it is verified in personal experience. This verification is affirmative: "This Way is a way to peace." As affirmative, it is not exclusive. The possibility remains that it is the only way to peace, a possibility often maintained and one we must consider. Here I simply point out that the verifying experience does not contain in itself any assertion to the effect that other ways are false: it implies no rejection of the vision of the true mystic wherever found, if there be any other true mystic— a doubt which followers of Christ have at times expressed, but which Christ himself was free from. And the word of him whom I have called the unbound Christ appears to reject any such rejection: he who stands and has stood at the door of every man must have done so under various guises.

Let me repeat that what I mean by "the true mystic" is simply the person who in the course of his own experience has in some moment become aware of the nature of things as supreme good. The awareness of Being, which is incessant and inescapable but almost always obscured by "the ten thousand things," comes abruptly to clarity unmixed. At some point he has broken through the illusions of mental habit; he has perceived that the apparent finality of the physical detail of experience is unreal, that the seemingly independent "fact" is dependent, that Being in its truth is Beatitude and kindred to himself. Such vision may come wholly outside the lines of formal religion, as it came to John Masefield—purely as "illumination" replacing "a black night of despair." [1] Or it may come in the way of

[1] *So Long to Learn,* 139, 180.

meditative discipline, as it may have come to Plotinus or to Plato. Or still more simply and widely, in the waking of the mind to love and the opening of the eyes to beauty, when these experiences are, as they may be, entrance gates to the nature of Being.

In the Orient and especially in India this experience is often deliberately sought under the name of "realization." Indeed, India while in many ways the most speculative and imaginative of all cultures in the field of religion, is also the most empirical in this sense of seeking an experience of union with the divine, and of making extraordinary efforts and sacrifices for its attainment. As contrasted with Christianity, the religions of India commonly encourage a spiritual athleticism in which realization is felt to be earned by personal effort, whereas for the Christian it is, in the end, felt to be a gift of grace. In India, too, the divine is often regarded as beyond personality, and union therewith a merging and loss of separate selfhood; whereas for the Christian the discovery is one of being prized as a person by a person. And further, while for the Indian mystic the achievement of *samadhi* may tend to remove him from the world of affairs as a world of Maya, and may culminate in his final release from illusion and from rebirth, it belongs to the genius of Christian mysticism that its realization is a phase of an alternation which makes him a revitalized participant in the historic work of the kingdom of God on earth.

But these contrasts are relative. There is nothing more personal than the religion of Tagore, a Brahma Samaj Hinduism, whose "religion of man" tends to find the divine encounter through such human offices as those of the *guru*. Tagore is doubtless influenced by his knowledge of Christianity, but even more by a type of people's mysticism current in parts of Bengal, that of the Baüls (many of whose songs he has set to music), who believe that they will meet the divine One in person, in some incidental human encounter, and will at the end join "Him" beyond humanity:

> And Thou, with what name wilt Thou call me?
> Thou wilt lift me from the water,
> And there, under the shelter of Thine arm,
>   Close to Thy heart,
> Wilt extinguish the burning of the long, long journey.

As for the motive of escape, certainly more prominent in the orthodoxies of Buddhism and Hinduism, we must recall that if the Enlightenment of the Buddha, according to the legend which everyone knows, led to his deliberately putting away the call of Nirvana because of his compassion for unenlightened mankind, Buddhism cannot be disposed of as "the Way of Escape": it is also the Denial of Escape as ultimate good, a denial repeated by the succession of Bodhisattvas. And if this is true of original Buddhism, the developed Mahayana of today is still more a call to man to find worth in human living by developing the Buddha nature within each one.

These several variants of mystic experience are thus not incompatible. All of them, including that of the Christian, call for a certain discipline,[2] and for a certain removal for recollection from the immediate strain of affairs, as a phase of alternation. All of them, including the most technical—as Yoga or Zen—and the most untechnical and spontaneous—the initiation into Being of which human love is capable—normally bring a healing gift of the same

---

[2] The earlier Christian enthusiasm sought a discipline more deliberate and systematic than at present. A reviewer of P. W. Martin's *Experiment in Depth* regrets that "spiritual exercises in the West have progressively atrophied during the 2000 years of Christendom." *Times Literary Supplement*, Sept. 2, 1955, 513.

nature: a gift of recovered sense of proportion, of certitude of will, of re-creation, the restored *pou sto* of aboriginal consciousness:

> This, and the child's unheeded dream
> Are all the light of all their day.

Whatever their departures from one another in practice and theory, there is a tendency for the mystics in various traditions—selectively—to understand one another. Would it not be the glory of a truly universal religion to lead into a single stream all these currents of integration and cure, so far as they are genuine?

The barrier is as obvious as the goal is inviting. It is that the mystic experience lacks words. It is often called "ineffable" by the mystic himself. Yet, as unvocal intuition, if it means anything at all it admits and requires interpretation—the mystic who refuses the offices of reason opposes his own gift—the integration of human nature. And while these variants may aid in interpreting one another, all interpretation proceeds at a risk. And the variant results appear to call for reinterpretation. How can modern man find his rational way amid their diversity, or tolerate their aberrations?

ii. *Three Postulates for the Relations of Religions*

THE relations between the several religions will be helped toward clarity if we observe the following forces constantly in play. We may state them as a set of postulates:

(a) The true mystic will recognize the true mystic across all boundaries, and will learn from him;

(b) Every man's religion must be "a" religion, having

its own simplicity of essence, its organic integrity, and its
historic identity;

(c) To every man belongs the full truth of religion—
the unlosable essences in whatever context they appear,
and also their interpretation through history.

We consider each of these postulates:

(a) *The true mystic will recognize the true mystic.* It
is all but fruitless to seek for criteria. There is, indeed, a
broad pragmatic test, "by their fruits." The objective
observer, being devoid of "the ear to hear," has to use this
test, and so the state. The test is useful especially in its
negative form: if the fruit is idleness, sensuality, disorder,
the mysticism is fraudulent. Mass movements against a
monastic life deemed parasitical and barren, as in the
sweeping revolts against early Buddhism in China and in
the disorders in England long ago, along the Scottish
border, suggest the common human basis for this judgment. In a still broader sense, in so far as the religions of
Asia have been, in fact, an opiate of the people, and have
deferred the rational attack on poverty, the powerful element of mysticism in them is suspect of imperfect definition. And at the same time, this mysticism is near to its
greatest service, the source of a cosmic patience and faith
that has sustained the hearts of millions under a persistent
privation which they, the common people, had no way to
remedy.[3] But the relevant and positive test is immediate: it
lies in the spirit of the man; in his attainment of
peace.

Gandhi was often invited to declare himself a Christian;
he was such in spirit and effect; he consistently and kindly
declined on the ground that "God had placed him in
India," and he could do much for Hinduism by working

[3] See my book, *Experiment in Education*, 159 f.

from within, as indeed he did. But one day (I am told) an English churchman who had argued the subject with him came to the final question: "Have you attained peace?" When Gandhi answered, "I have peace," the reply was, "Then I have nothing more to say to you." The direct recognition by Irwin and Gandhi of the true mystic, each in the other, has been important for the peaceful character of the great turn of Indian history in 1947. But the recognition I speak of may be as well illustrated in events almost trifling and momentary.

> North of Hangchow there was in 1932 a new Taoist temple, founded by a Cantonese merchant who desired to restore Taoism to its original purity. I found there an old gardener, keeping a loving eye and hand on his plantings; and in the entire absence of a common language had a few words with him. I knew that his plants were to him a manifestation of the Tao, whose polar factors, Yang and Yin, entered into all living things. As he spoke of them, I have seldom seen so beautiful a human face, inlighted with a sense of communing with the source of the life that was in his keeping. Through his garden-tending he was doing what Lao Tze called "returning to the root": we might call it prayer, in the sense of the Benedictine for whom *laborare est orare*.

With such recognition, wherever it occurs, there comes at least a readier disposition—perhaps a sort of mandate—to discern convergence, under wide differences of expression, in the meaning of essences and observances among different faiths.

Even the great induction of Christianity, he that loseth his life for my sake the same shall find it, even this master precept nowhere else so radically and compactly expressed, ceases to stand alone. Indeed, as we noted, it would hardly be so persuasive an essence unless some inkling of its purport had been widely felt.

It has some kinship with the universal symbol of *renunciation as a condition of insight*, sometimes taking the physical form of austerity as a preparation for worship. In all religions, the capacity for renunciation has been honored as a sign of spiritual power; it has contributed to the influence of a Gandhi, as well as of a Francis or a Savonarola. Its root does not lie in vocal convention: wherever spiritual ambition appears, some spontaneous curbing of natural impulse occurs as an intuitively felt condition of the life-saving subordination of instinct. It is understood by Spinoza as clearly as by Augustine.

I had long supposed that Confucius, recommending a "Middle Path" as a primary moral principle, lacked an understanding of the firm radicalism of self-sacrifice, characteristic of the Christian absolutes. (And since it is only in presence of such absolutes that any man can judge his own moral status, their relative absence from any tradition might account for a prevalent once-born-ness to which a sense of sin could seem alien.) But I have recently come on a phrase that throws light on the inner greatness of the aging master in his courageous persistence, despite repeated failure and occasional physical assault, in the effort to persuade local rulers to good government. The phrase *"Ssu ming lun,"* which Wing-tsit Chan translates "Waiting for the Heavenly Mandate," [4] may be interpreted "Accepting without complaint whatever fortune may attend the carrying-out of one's Heaven-appointed task"— many words for a brief Chinese phrase, but that is the nature of brief Chinese phrases! Mencius comments that this loyal persistence may involve death. And certainly, the danger-defying dedication of Confucius to his teaching mission, like that of Socrates, has been a potent factor in

[4] Chan Wing-tsit, *Religious Trends in Modern China*, 29.

the enduring aliveness of his message.[5] The principle of losing life to save it is there.

And I know of no other great tradition in which there is not a latent acceptance or adumbration of this principle, not yet given the place of priority that belongs to it. So far as this is the case Christianity, through its inductive power, may provide an interpretation by whose aid these approaches may be reconceived within their own context. And they, in turn, will provide for the Christian dictum a reconception in terms of breadth: the Christian will know better what his own precept means as he sees its identity under widely different conceptual auspices, such as those of the Chinese *Ming*, the Mandate of Heaven.

The intuitive recognition of mystic by mystic is thus the perceptive clue through which the formidable oppositions between the great positive religions are to some extent bridged. Their incompatibilities are reduced to their residual dimensions. The age before us will be to just that extent relieved of unreal contentions or estrangements. And few things discredit the position of organized religion in the mind of modern man so much as artificial or verbal antagonisms on the part of the one association devoted to the moral unity of mankind.

Not all incompatibilities will be thus disposed of; but this process of reduction will enable us to define the residue, and to assess their future.

(b) *Every man's religion must be "a" religion, having its own simplicity of essence and its own integrity*, averse to the harboring of inwardly discordant or superfluous elements.

[5] *Philosophy East and West*, IV, 2 (July, 1954), 179–81, a review of Chan's book by Richard and W. E. Hocking.

Since the mystic's recognition of the true mystic is limited by no conceptual boundaries, it is *prima facie* at odds with the idea that any one confession is the "Only Way" of finding God. If this be "Liberalism," it is but God's own liberalism, whose light "lighteth every man." But it cannot serve as our sole guide.

For if we thereupon say that all ways are good ways, and add (as Ramakrishna inclined to do) that all ways are equally good, we fall into an Indifferentism that evades deep-going issues. And if we say that each man's religion is the right way *for him*, despite material divergences, we adopt a Relativism equally negligent, and which has nothing to offer to a coming world order committed to a pursuit of universal truth, in religion as in science. Science itself has a sort of "Only Way"—its method: as Dewey points out, "There is but one sure road of access to truth— the road of patient, cooperative enquiry." [6] Likewise the Only Way position in religion has at least the similar merit of rejecting passivity before crucial issues of truth and error, valid faith and superstition, right and wrong, if such issues exist. As they do.

The Only Way in religion has a further merit, that of intolerance toward a Syncretism which is disposed to borrow here and there what seems to be good, encouraged no doubt by the mystic's recognition, piecing together fragments of true insight from various sources to compose an eclectic whole, devoid of any principle of coherence. I do not mean that such patchwork borrowing is wrong: if something is found good, it is already yours; you cannot disown it. The way to an honest breadth must begin with such borrowing, as it were a tentative syncretism. But it must *come to unity* with whatever else you have. A man's

[6] Dewey, *op. cit.*, 32.

religion must be *one thing,* in the sense of having a central essence which commands all else. Your borrowing, then, must be the beginning of a thinking process. Either that good thing you have found belongs uniquely to the religious organism from which it came—in which case you must adopt *that* unity—or it belongs to *yours*—in which case you must *reconceive* the essence of your own faith, to include that new element.[7] You cannot live religiously within a divided house, or a house whose roof covers only part of its floor area!

This demand for integrity is intuitive as well as logical. Whether or not the priests and theologians of any faith are able to reach agreement as to what the essence of the faith is, the individual adherent, as he pronounces the sacred name or "takes refuge in the Dharma," must be able to feel himself at one in thought and spirit not only with fellow adherents but also with the saints in that tradition through the ages of its history. For this reason, a Gandhi, so much in accord with Christianity in precept and action, could not find this accord a sufficient reason for separation from Hinduism: his deeper intuitions were there—he said to me that the name "Rama" remained to him the most intimate and significant of the names of God —and he believed he could reach unity by incorporating his new insights within the body of a reinterpreted Hinduism. To achieve this, he so radically reconceived Hinduism as to call forth fierce hostility in some centers of strict Hindu orthodoxy. Finally his integrity cost him his life.

It is just this necessary insistence on inner unity that leaves us with a plurality of integral faiths. If postulate

[7] This is the specific process of "reconception" which I have earlier defined as the unit step in the growing process of every living religion, its dialectic in which faith co-operates with thought. *Living Religions and a World Faith,* 190–98.

one tends to bring the religions together, postulate two tends to confirm their separate outlines. Are we then committed to an enduring plurality of religions, each aspiring to universal scope, and each held by its center to be the Only Way?

(c) *To every man belongs the full truth of religion*— the unlosable essences in whatever context they appear, and their interpretation through history.

The destinies of religion in the age now arriving will not be governed chiefly by the findings of scholars or priests, but rather by what men everywhere seek as filling their need for an inner peace. To every man, the West and the East alike will naturally contribute whatever is universal in their cultures, no longer as western or eastern, but as his own. This, which already holds of the sciences, holds in principle of religion also, though what is universal in religion is made less available by the diversities we are dealing with, and their various geographical centers of diffusion. It is well to note that the plurality that results is largely illusory.

So far as the essences of precept and doctrine are concerned, the agreements which the mystics discern are *not similarities, they are identities*. Each man in following the Way of his faith is, of course, regarding that Way as universal—otherwise it would not be his faith. His religion is his private self-dedication to Being, which is one, and therewith his bond to the ideal community of mankind. Consciously or not, each one is seeking not "a" Way, but the "Only Way": just as any scientist is concerned to have not "a" truth, but The Truth, so the worshiper in whatever name will consider his way the Only Way, not as a proprietary nostrum but as The Truth indivisible and The Life, and as universal for just that reason. And con-

versely, whatever else in religion is universal is *ipso facto*
part of it, and his own.

Thus understood, the Only Way, so far as its essence has
by valid induction achieved finality, is no longer the Way
that marks out one religion from all others: it is the Way
already present in all, either explicitly or *in ovo.* The several universal religions *are already fused together, so to
speak, at the top.*[8] The primary identity involved in the
recognition of mystic by mystic is the essence of the religious world view, the perception of Being as beatitude—
God is, and God is One. With this final and universal truth
whatever is implied in it, and that is much, is already implicitly the possession of every believer within his own
faith. And as we have just seen, there is wide identity in
a major essence of precept. So far, the religions of mankind—Buddhism not excluded—are already one religion. The area of this agreement-and-unity is subject to
continuous enlargement by the processes of mystic recognition and reconception.

The recognition that there are finalities in religion is
the condition under which alone the unity of religion is
not only a hope, but in some measure an actuality. The
usual "Only Way" doctrine has the special virtue, in an
era of mental flabbiness, of recognizing that there is such
a thing as finality within our reach, such as we have indicated in the unlosable intuitions of Christianity. The Flux-
philosophers who find nothing not subject to change, and
who in the field of religion can provide no firm center of
assurance in the increasingly grave problem of motivation,
have something to learn from the Only Way proponent.
The region of the changeless need not be great. I am in
mind of a remark by Royce reported by Max Otto when

[8] See above, p. 138.

someone asked him the object of his teaching: "I wish to give my students a little place on which to set their feet" —a spot of stability in a world of change. If religion gives its whole content over to the principle *panta rei*, it has surrendered its major function.

iii. *The Positive Religions Retain Marks of Distinction*

BUT there remain the historical and personal factors unaffected by these *rapprochements*.

Regional histories have long since merged in a world history; but the several courses of experience that have formed the vital arguments of development within the various faiths remain as distinct as the persons of their founders. And if the history of a religion is a factor in its definition, diversities of history cannot but imply continuing diversities of essence.

Further, these histories of religion have been at the same time deeply involved with the histories of culture. They have been engaged in the molding of customs and laws, of myth and of art, and especially of *observance*—a language beyond language whose field is extensive and strangely durable. There are the holy days, modes of prayer, taboos, charms, magic techniques, feasts, special ceremonies to note the vital crises, birth, maturity, marriage, death, sacraments, invocations of special powers for community crises and the major enterprises of the economic year.

In brief, particular religion is the leaven of the spirit of tribes and nations. Its observances can with difficulty be kept to one side of the religious-secular boundary: witness the vast public (and commercial) import of the Christmas holiday, the stamping of the European business calendar

by the Christian week and yearly festivals whose momen-
tum carries far beyond the Christian world, as in the ac-
commodation of Turkish bank holidays to those of Europe
. . . Religion, I say, permeates the spirit of nations; and
nationhood, with all its past crimes and its peril for future
world unity, *is not destined to disappear.*

Here I am obliged to record dissent from the outlook
of Toynbee, and from that of many another messenger of
good will to men, including Albert Einstein, appalled by
the horrors let loose on the world by the egoism of nation-
states, and by the far greater horrors now at the service of
political passion. My dissent is based on the judgment
that just because civilization is becoming one and world-
wide, the localisms which preserve the world from monot-
ony, and conserve those precious semi-solitudes in which
alone thought and fine art and every creative impulse
flourish, must be the more vigorously protected and prized.
And these nationalisms, normally held from excess by the
growing effectiveness of the world-wide treasury of the
universal, in science, economy, law, faith, are inseparable
from the local history of religion.

As evidence, consider the new national impulses of Asia
and their bearing on ancient faiths. Just now, Buddhism
and Hinduism in India, long in decline, are again lifting
their heads.[9] Japan's experience is peculiarly instructive,
since its phenomenal commitment to modernity and its un-

[9] "Hinduism and Buddhism are by no means dead in India. They . . .
are proclaiming themselves today as the new hope of humanity" (D. G.
Moses, *Christian Century,* Mar. 30, 1955). This statement recalls the
welcome given by Pandit N. N. DasGupta at the opening of the
Buddhist temple at Sarnath, Sept., 1931: a welcome to the coming
"Hindu-Buddhist civilization of India," and of Asia. The hyphen marks
a burial of ancient hostilities between these faiths—a burial hardly con-
ceivable prior to World War I which published to the East a breach in
Christendom, to DasGupta "a failure" of Christianity.

paralleled rapidity of secular adaptation might have
tended to obliterate its sympathy with tradition. Instead,
Japan some time ago devised a new relationship to religious
tradition: it adhered to Shinto as a national outlook, carefully distinguished (by official definition) from religious-
and-sectarian Shinto; and this adherence, with its corresponding observances, was in my opinion an important
factor in the notable nonreceptivity, prior to the recent
war, of the Japanese public to the spread of antinational-
ist communism.[10] The effectiveness of Shinto in this respect
comes not from any doctrinal formula, and certainly not
from specific divine figures, but from the rootage of the
distinctive Japanese culture—its art, love of nature, custom, heroic ideals . . . in the symbols of Shinto tradition.

There is here no wish to preserve from passing that
which is outworn—as Shinto's involvement with a hier-
archical social order, already distasteful to Japanese youth
—nor to hold in the position of literal faith that which is
moving and ought to move into the region of myth. The
acids of modernity will quietly do their own work. But we
can and must treat with reverence the unanalyzed sources
of the individuality of historic cultures. We must respect
the enduring germ of vitality in what Royce called "the
We," whose quasi-personal being is a factor in the selfhood
of each member-person. To say of these older religions, as
suggested by an Evanston report, that they "have no
message of abiding hope" is to utter a judgment that
might be drawn from comparing texts, but never from
considering the hearts of common men long sustained by
these faiths. They, too, the folk, are among the mystics.

[10] The present postwar period in which Japan is drawn powerfully
into sympathy with Asian antiwesternism has a radically different
balance.

When nationalism becomes itself a religion, or when the church identifies itself with the interests of the state, true religion is dead. In the civilization now coming, there is no more place for "national religions" than for chosen people. Nor is any national character or temperament permanent; ancient observances have a tendency to outlive the meanings that begot them. The fortunate plasticity of nationhood is a condition of the swift growths and swift sharings of culture involved in the reaching of a world civilization. Yet *for any epoch, there is such a thing as national personality, and therewith national mission.* The nation-group can lend a necessary touch of domesticity to the law-making association, whereby the total positive law of that group becomes a distinctive experiment in living. Through this genuine, even if passing, personal quality, ideas are born, inherently universal. It is only in the relatively secret places of the world that creativity takes place for the renewal of the life of all. Religion will therefore always have two functions in reference to this national being: that of transcending all national limits, and that of maintaining with loving piety the permanent values of domesticity in the interior groupings of mankind.[11]

For a world civilization must be an organism, not an endless homogeneity. No more desolating prospect could confront mankind than that of undifferentiated identity in the sacred begettings of culture. The quest for a world faith must retain, in its care for the whole, a continuing solicitude for its diverse members. And not alone for the sake of the worshipers whose ancestral reverences are involved, but also for the sake of that total human experience to which belongs the full truth of religion.

[11] Hocking, *Man and the State*, 267, 372; *The Spirit of World Politics*, 186 f., 194.

Our three postulates for the interrelation of faiths have brought us to no goal, working as they have to some extent at cross-purposes. They have led us to the perception that an incipient world faith already exists, though not in the shape of "a" religion positive and historic. The immediate vista for the coming civilization is that of a continued coexistence of at least a few of the great faiths.

This coexistence can no longer be one of mutual effort for displacement. The advance toward a world cultivation proceeds under a disposition close to the essence of all civilization which we may call *reverence for reverence*— something far away from toleration—with the general insight that no soul through defects in the particulars of its faith stands apart from the mercy of God.

This does not mean that abuses in religion are not to be noted and given their right names. Whatever makes religion important makes its aberrations the more deplorable, and the more traitorous to the common quest; for in a civilization of increasing general enlightenment and humanism, positive religion always faces the issue of its own existence. The worship of idols has always to be denounced in plain terms. Nor is this worship less prevalent now than in ancient days: it is more so. The advance of civilization but changes its form; for it lies in the nature of civilization to deify its man-made winnings. There is no civilization in which the admonition of the Hindu mystic is not needed: *Neti, neti*—"it is not that!" There is no achieved good which is not invited to pose as The Good—liberty, equality, the standard of living, democracy, the nation itself, good fortune and the benevolence of the fortunate—all such goods stand on the perilous slope toward a false absolutism. And it is always the office of religion to refuse the place of perfection to the near-perfect. In this sense its

God is *always a jealous God*: his jealousy is identical with his stern love for the soul's purity.

Hatred of the idol as god-pretender, legitimate and necessary passion of original Judaism, does not of itself today set one religion against another nor justify a self-righteous separatism; for this hatred is in the lifeblood of every living religion. It is *the domestic issue for every reformer.* Wherever we recognize this holy austerity, whether in Buddha or Jesus or al-Hallaj or Gandhi or others, there speaks, or should speak, our reverence for reverence. At the same time the coexistence of the great faiths cannot be passive; that would be to fall into the Indifferentism we are bound to reject. The claim of each to universal meaning implies a universal responsibility; and since religion does not, like science, universalize itself, it implies a duty to "go and preach." If we break the images of idolatry within our own house, and solely for our own private good-standing with the God of truth, we have set up a new idol in doing so. How, then, can coexistence be other than contentious, and in a sense competitive?

Here we reach the crux of our meditation.

iv. *Immediate Considerations:*
Individual Freedom; Consociation

TOWARD this conflict of duties, our actual situation, there are two considerations of direct pertinence, and two further considerations presiding over the ultimate issue. First, for the immediate situation:

With the invasion of the spirit of modernity into all crannies of the planet, religion by group-belonging becomes less and less possible to the man who thinks; and the

man who thinks tends to become everyman.[12] We have to
consider the *intense individuality* of the address of religion
today and of all future religion. There is still a tendency
of organized religion to regard itself as having a *domain*
like that of the nation or the region, like that of the
Moslem world or the Roman Catholic districts of Europe
or South America. And where religion places its hand
directly on legislation, that tendency has a concrete *raison
d'être*, limiting individual freedom to choose through the
force of a well-defined *esprit de corps*. But here the gains
of modernity in the West become the general principle of
the new era: it is not westernism but universal necessity
that religion in its nature must speak to the individual
soul. In the last analysis a religion has no domain, other
than that of the heart's peace; and the individual heart is
the sole judge of its own peace, and of its need for further
search. Here freedom must be absolute; and must be ab-
solutely protected, not alone for the weal of the person,
but as well for the solidity of civilization.

We must also consider that *the impulse to teach is inseparable from the impulse to learn*, and learning, in religion, means experiencing. Wherever the reverence for
reverence exists there will be a willingness to worship with
the worshiper, as Gandhi, the Hindu, was willing to worship with the Christian. Each faith has its unlosables,
which can best be understood by experimental adoption,
not so much in the spirit of Keyserling's dramatic inquiries
as in that of the more serious devotions of Ramakrishna or
of Augustine's *credo ut intelligam*.

Count Hermann von Keyserling in his *Travel Diary*

[12] A tendency suffering check in regions where, as in the United
States, mass education is mistaken for democracy in education.

indicates that understanding a faith requires a sort of Protean self-identification with it, *for a time*; he relates how for a day or two he "adopted the belief" in Krishnamurti as a contemporary incarnation, just to see how it would feel to believe that! Much more genuine do I find this statement of a Jesuit missionary in India: "India's problems I had studied . . . I read books, but the books I liked the most were the hearts of the people I dealt with, especially the simple and the ignorant. . . . I meditated over the memorials of the birthplaces of Buddhism and Jainism, and sat in the caves used by a sect of monks with no spiritual descendants in the world of today. . . . I let children and illiterates teach me, and they nearly made me feel the value of their superstitions. . . ." But most to our present point is the attitude I met in Professor Adhikari, of the Hindu University of Benares, who finding the doctrine of this same Jesuit missionary as to transubstantiation difficult, said to him, "We must go together to your Mary-chapel and pray there; and perhaps the understanding will come to me." Without losing grip on the firm identity of his own Way, each can grow in his understanding of that Way through the added experience of worship with another in whom the reality of religion is perceived. Each will thereby reconceive his own faith in breadth. And with the breaking down of the surface shells of insulation, the natural reasons for preference and decision will assert themselves.

As the recognition of kinship between different faiths becomes general, while the call of historical loyalty remains strong, occasional acts of co-worship may develop freely into what I have called "consociation," [13] as in the "Wider

[13] In my article, "Missions in a Nationalist Orient," *Christian Century*, Feb. 23, 1955.

Christian Fellowship" which once flourished in India, and to some extent in the new association of "National Churches" in India. And consociation, as a limited union between faiths for work and worship, is a definite step toward making the visible institutions more truthfully express the realities of identity within difference, moving toward difference within identity.

v. *Long-range Considerations: Maturity in Religion*

BUT for the longer look ahead there are two further considerations. These arise from the fact that as the one civilization establishes itself, with the practical insistence of technical and economic issues, the strong drift to a common scientific and secular outlook, the disappearance of the older colonial structures and the corresponding necessities for cultural self-sufficiency everywhere, the traditional problems of religion will tend to be submerged under the common problems of the new order. Young people will be keenly aware of the life-and-death issues which all religion faces, as modernity presents itself as a good in itself. There arises a new perspective on all religious theses and observances.

One consideration of this new perspective is a recognition of *the necessity and incomparable worth of maturity in religion.*

The coming of the new perspective has shown itself, among the religions of Asia, in a swift adoption, as in the *gurukuls* of India, as in Al Azhar, Aligarh, and other Moslem centers of learning, of new curricula including the sciences together with literatures and philosophies aiming to orient the mind of man within a radically altered world picture. However successful these efforts, they will almost by necessity fall short of *maturity*.

By maturity I mean here something more than several centuries of encounter with the modern outlook. I mean a *union of opposites*, such as maturity in organic life implies, in which the world views of religion have absorbed and made their own what is valid in the views of its critics. A religion that remains hostile to nature *per se* or to the scientific spirit is simply not mature; nor is a religion mature that merely accepts science and retreats, priding itself on its up-to-dateness, its realism, its ability to wear sociological garments. Maturity means the glad and intelligent adoption *of the natural, without the surrender of what is more than nature*, as the human mind, which thinks nature, obeys nature in its empirical inquiries, and thus masters nature, is other and more than the nature which is its "object." It means recognizing that this *being-above-nature is also natural*, i.e., it is "human nature" to be the knower of (object) nature and the free utilizer of (object) nature. And for this reason the term "nature" is seen to have two meanings, or two boundaries, one of which is limited to the sphere of events within the given space-time-causal nexus, and one of which includes with this the sphere of human thought, purpose, and freedom, with whatever wider environment these imply.

There is a "nature" that excludes supernature; *there is a wider "nature" which includes supernature,*[14] and can therefore do justice to the nonphysical realities, such as life, consciousness, man, history, the universal, the eternal. Mature religion, continuing like all religion to denounce avarice, lust, the indulgence of wrath, and the will to dominate, will at the same time assert the justice of natural

[14] See above, pp. 102f.

instinct when held subordinate to a ruling passion of a
creative love (also natural *in posse*). In rebuking nature
it will honor nature, finding in nature itself the standards
for the rebuke of nature.

The great men of all ages have found within their own
natures something that controls and disciplines nature.
The astonishing outburst of Tertullian above referred to,
"O testimonium animae naturaliter Christianae" (*Apolo-
geticus*, XVII), was preceded by a reflection less often
noticed, indicating *the ground* upon which he felt he could
assert that the human mind is Christian by nature. That
ground seems to me at least as astonishing in its context as
the implied assertion. If I rightly interpret his compact
phrases, he says in effect that *our knowledge* that we cannot fully grasp the ultimate Being affords evidence that
we have *a place in knowledge* for what it is that we cannot
grasp. And this place is so important that he can add, *Et
haec est summa delicti nolentium recognoscere, quem ig-
norare non possunt*—"And this is the highest reach of
wrong—the unwillingness to recognize what it is impossible to ignore." In other words, to know that we cannot
know may be our most significant knowledge, the item most
perilous to repudiate. This bit of irony—which we now
incline to call dialectic—is of a piece with the paradox of
Socrates, whose point of superior wisdom was that he alone
knew his ignorance. And this, in turn, is of a piece, in quite
different language, with the Hebrew dictum, "the fear of
the Lord is the beginning of wisdom"—if we consider "the
Lord" as the eternal knower of what we do not know, as
well as the Absolute Being, the ever-present yet inaccessible
goal of our own knowing. And if "fear" means the reverent
regard (like the mystic's "mystery") for the ontological
implication of this so-naturally-human knowledge of the

numen beyond knowing, our link to beyond-human entity. Maturity in this sense will become a need for all religion. For with the growing unity of civilization, the mental environment of all religions will contain (to use Toynbee's terms) the same new challenges, and will call for the same responses on their part. This demand will press—is already pressing—toward simplicity and a care for stark veracity *beneath the indispensable poetry*; and this can only make for convergence of the several great religions on certain common essentials. The problem of religious knowledge, sharpened by the universal acute self-consciousness of scientific method, compels a community even of language in the defense of any faith whatever. The mystic everywhere must *know* whereon he stands.

In this common emergency—for such it is—there is but one of the great religions whose history has driven it to an approximate maturity. There is but one that has been compelled to come to terms with a nationally convincing and technically triumphant naturalism, with the mind-body realism from which modernity springs, with a psychology of great prowess, value, and depth which can implicitly present a human nature devoid of freedom in plausible defiance of what everyone knows, with a social science whose strong and valid sense of relativity is prepared to sweep away every absolute as mischievous arrogance, including those absolutes on which its own judgments of relativity must be based. I will not say that Christianity is unitedly equipped with the answers. I will say that the answers are at hand within its immediate context and are being recognized. And it becomes, therefore, the opportunity—not the boast—of Christianity to lend its maturity to all religions.

This unique position of Christianity, which it would be

unjust to attribute solely to accidents of its history, since that history of encounter with well-armed critics is largely of its own breeding, will not be unfelt by alert minds among Oriental youth. It will result, in those objective enough to distinguish the religion from its associations with political westernisms substantially outgrown, in a new consideration of Christianity as of a needed source of strength, such as we have noted above on the part of certain Japanese thinkers (p. 120). Indeed, in so far as the world faith for the arriving civilization must be a mature faith, finding its way to a natural union of the natural and the supernatural, it is possible to say that this religion under whatever name will necessarily be in substance Christian.

vi. *Long-range Considerations: Spiritual Iron; Auspicious Fanaticism*

BUT maturity is not the sole long-distance consideration. There is an equally permanent necessity for what I will call *spiritual iron*, with which maturity by itself is not necessarily in harmony. Here Christianity, in its modern phase, has something to learn not alone from the contemporary, but also from the more ancient East. For there is a certain danger that the Orient, under the pressure of swiftly growing hopes and the labors of social reconstruction, may loosen its hold on its own unique ancient sources of strength.

Where can we find today that incomparable continuity of high discipline and mental prowess that could transmit *memoriter* a vast tradition as this has been done in India? The arrival of a "New Dispensation" has always been a signal for dissolving former observances and types of training; and they are often due for dissolving, but not for the dismissal of their intensity of commitment and energy of aspiration. There remains in the East a distinctive moral virility of which all religion has persistent need, particularly a religion which, like much current Christianity, tends to regard itself as a fortunately conceived synthesis of both worlds. For current Christianity, precisely through its growing capacity to bring nature and supernature together into organic union—well cured of rigors formerly inspired by fears of Hell, and equally unenticed by such images as those of Dante's or Milton's Paradise—tends to find in its sagacious synthesis, not that nature is lifted up but that supernature is reduced to a humanistic affix of nature. Prior to the present era of possible human self-destruction on a world scale, with its abrupt demand for literal truth-facing, there had entered a certain complacency into the Christian outlook. This complacency was ready to translate sin as an indisposition open to psychiatric treatment, to regard the Cross as an outgrown medieval emblem, to consider human suffering as the unfinished business of applied science, and, except for a few heroic spirits, too spiritually and mentally weary to assume the growing burden of a technically competent world's underlying doubt and despair.

This same Christianity which once gave the western world a revolutionary concept, the right of the responsible individual against the state, and *fought for it*,[15] seems as a body too flabby to protest when that priceless treasure is transmuted into an unconditional birthday present for

---

[15] Cf. Tertullian's fearless assertion of the right to choose one's own religion.

each sentient seeker of his personal happiness. The will to create through suffering is damped down into the will to have a costless comfort.

There *is no costless comfort* to be had in this world, still less a costless joy. For there is no satisfaction of the will apart from work done—in the end, of taking a share in world-making, whether as farmer or mechanic, as home-maker or law-maker. . . . No artist can make without travail an honest report of what soul he finds in things. Not even love can come to its own without pain; for loving or being loved is no right already paid for by existent merit or beauty; it is a glory undeserved, unseekable, and calling for life service. And wherever love is made cheap, there is the cheapness of a civilization's soul. If the East has needed the technical steel of the West, the West needs the spiritual iron of the East. For the East has never forgotten that there are conditions for our good, a moral law at the heart of the universe, even when conceived under the forbidding and imperfect guise of Karma.

We have been too easily satisfied to say that Christianity is the religion of love, without noting that the love of God toward man can be no regime of moral ease. If, as Buddha may have suspected, the unbending impersonality of the order of nature is the reliable imprint of an infinite care,[16] the converse is also true. Love—always more than law— must still speak through law,[17] the divine personality

---

[16] Whitehead suggests (*Science and the Modern World*, pp. 40f.) that the Christian conception of a detailed special Providence is a prelude to the modern conception of a minutely calculable physical law.

[17] My booklet, *Science and the Idea of God*, is essentially an essay on nonphysical law in the structure of experience. The religion of Buddha, often described as godless, has as its basis what Fichte—also accused of atheism—called the moral order of the universe. It would be more accurate to say that Buddhism resolves God as Being into God as Process, responsive to moral distinctions.

through impersonality over vast regions of its undeviating solicitude.

Arnold Toynbee calls the Christianity of today to "repentance" for its presumed monopoly of God's grace. Let me put it thus: our Christianity is in need of reconception through a deeper and humbler intercourse with the soul of the East, in its agelong acceptance of a searching self-discipline.

This call to learn from the East will be taking us nearer to the spirit of an earlier Christianity! There is no stronger endorsement of the lasting significance of the message emanating from Galilee than the fact that in moving forward past modernity we arrive at a better comprehension of its changeless demands. For the claims of the absolute and the perfect are not afflicted with age. In this sense it can be said that wherever man journeys, Christ as the voice of the absolute has been there before him! Fanaticism, if we distinguish between its types, has a permanent role in the world: in one type, the ruthless inhumanity of a Hitler; in another, the startling certitude of a Schweitzer rooted in a clear recognition of the claim of an "impossible" standard, first made articulate two thousand years ago. In this sense, the fanaticism of Christ is the perpetuity of his pertinence. The Orient has continued to understand this aspect of his teaching better than we.

Let us carry a step farther this meditation on fanaticism.[18]

---

[18] "Fanaticism" as a word which has lost caste may be beyond rescue. But it is fair to remember that the Latin *fanaticus* is simply the person who, in the spiritual atmosphere of the *fanum*, the temple, has becomé divinely inspired. The sacred madness shades into the unthinking rigidity and then into "possession" by the demon, which now usurps the name of fanaticism.

What has chiefly stood in the way of the message of the Nazarene in the Orient has been less the political and economic tempers of imperialism which have often accompanied its course, than a certain lack of contrition on the part of many of its messengers. For Christianity is not something we *have*, and can therefore transmit: it is something we have continually to seek, knowing that it is forever beyond us.

This lack of contrition is likely to result from a loss of the vision of an absolute demand, on the ground of a prudent perception that the absolute cannot be attained. To reduce one's aim to the dimension of the attainable is surely a counsel of good sense, perhaps of morality itself, if one would escape the condemnation of pursuing utopias, or of "idealism" as the crowning vice of dreamers from Plato onward. But the logic of the case, which is also its morality, is simple: if the standard which reports the true measure of our performance is not held in its full simplicity and force, the result will be the replacement of the true standard with something "fairly good." This is the new idolatry of which we have spoken, superseding the ancient idolatry of the image, willing like its ancestor to make a god of the best it has so far achieved. Thus our mastery of nature—surely God's will for man—our conquests of disease, of poverty, misery, ignorance, all these and other triumphs, tend to mount the stage one by one as The Good, rather than as the conditional goods they are, within the frame of the simple but unyielding requirement of the perfect-in-heart, without which they, too, contain the seeds of corruption.

It is part of the strange shallowness of recent western life that it should be deemed a conceit to recognize an absolute, and a humility to consider all standards relative, whereas it is precisely the reverse: it is only the absolute that duly rebukes our pride. And only a religion setting an absolute standard for the heart as well as for the will can carry the permanent cure for spiritual arrogance, while remaining—at whatever stage of our moral journey—still in advance. That religion, again under whatever name, is in its nature the Only Way.

Reinhold Niebuhr represents for our time the intense actuality of this dilemma. It is necessary, as he has so effectively shown, to see Christianity as pertinent to existing issues, and to recognize the inescapable sharing in the corporate guilt of every participant in community action. The possibilities, in modern society, of any incorporation of a clear ideal diminish; and as Hegel pointed out in his introduction to *Philosophie des Rechts*, the man who holds himself aloof from association with the imperfect not alone isolates himself, but plays the part of the destroyer. This almost axiomatic consideration tends to round off the practical maxims of the "good citizen" until, as the good-enough citizen, he loses his cutting edge. Holding to the great virtue of compromise, he becomes incapable of a creative fanaticism. He may become the notable civil servant, administrator, party leader; but he cannot reach—perhaps not understand—the sources of power in a Schweitzer or a Gandhi. He may become a Lord Lloyd, but never a Lord Irwin. I am prepared to say that the man of sense and conscience must always recognize the achievable, and work for it, but at the same time never confuse it with the morally requisite; he must keep both in view, as the marksman must see his target and at the same time allow for the drop of his bullet. In this sense, *Christianity is*

definable as a creative fanaticism, based on its prophecy
of the victorious power of forceless good will. To discount
its idealism is to destroy its essence.

vii. *The Goal of Confluence and the Ultimate Name*

NEITHER of these two long-range demands upon the
future world religion—neither maturity nor an inspired
radicalism—is likely to be borrowed or transferred from
religion to religion. Both represent qualities which the
religious sense of mankind will increasingly crave in its
historic faiths, and which will be absorbed degree by
degree as these faiths interact with the ripening insights
of their own communicants. The spiritual iron of the East,
as a nonlocal factor of human dignity, never complete,
will be likely to come by way of periods of public crisis,
bringing revulsion against the self-satisfied urbanities of
polite religion, and a thirst for that natural greatness—
the special province of religion—for which first things are
put first, as in the days when the blood of martyrs was
indeed the seed of the church, and the salt of the earth had
not lost its savor.

These processes will therefore promote the silent *rapprochement* of the great faiths, without canceling the
differences in historic rootage. The Christian will not be
concerned that the total outlook slowly emerging bear his
name. He will be mindful that his Master in one parable
likened the kingdom of God to leaven which a woman took
and hid in three measures of meal till the whole was
leavened—the hidden anonymity a favorable condition for
its work. The time is ripe for that radical reconception of
which we have spoken, whereby the concept of the Christ
is extended to include that unbound Spirit who stands and

has stood at the door of every man, and who, in various guises, still appears to him who opens, both as an impersonal word and as a personal presence. As such a presence, he relieves at a stroke that sense of the measureless vastness of the world in which the individual soul finds itself a negligible atom, hopelessly lost. It is this, intrinsically incredible, personal address of the immensities of the cosmos and of history—the necessary and sufficient answer to the quantitative revelations of astrophysics [19]—which, I surmise, will tend to identify the resulting world faith.

But the specific name will not be insisted upon, it will be chosen. This reconception would involve putting away an inherently noble but limiting type of Only-Way Christianity whose impulse to spread the faith has been less the joy of good tidings than the rescue motive, hoping to avert a prospect of damnation hanging over the souls of those unredeemed by a personal disclosure of the strait gate and narrow way. When we put away the essentially superstitious idea that there is one official divine-human administration of the entrance into life, open to variation by plea, performance, or penance, rather than in the inherent arduousness of the conditions of human release into peace and greatness, the traditional Only-Way must yield to the Way which alone defines those conditions with truth and justice.[20] In such yielding, Christianity as an organization would lose a motive for propaganda based on special access to the "keys," but it would realize a far more convincing universality based on an application to itself of its own maxim, "He that loseth his life *for my sake*, the same shall find it."

[19] *Science and the Idea of God*, 112 ff.
[20] Perhaps implied in Radhakrishnan's remark: "The distressing feature of our age is not its atheism but its belief, the strange forms of superstition which it is willing to adopt." *Recovery of Faith*, 1955.

Retaining the symbols of their historic pieties, the great faiths will grow in their awareness of a unity more significant than the remaining differences. As an ancient Hindu tradition runs, the place of junction of rivers has a peculiar sanctity, because each of the streams then realizes its full being. But if Jumna and Ganges run together, shall the united lower stream be called Ganges or Jumna? Is it neither? Is it both? Or is it that one whose symbol men freely find compacted with the sense of both, holding in a historic life and deed, for which there can be no repetition and no substitute, a prophetic answer to man's eternal need?

NEWER VISTAS OF THOUGHT AND ACTION

i. *Necessity and Difficulty of Forecast:*
Its One Firm Ground

FARTHER than any other creature, man lives in the future; the effectiveness of his living depends on the sagacity of his forecast. He cannot evade the function of prophecy.

Yet the foreseeing of human affairs becomes increasingly hazardous. Laws of nature that support prediction in physics here lose footing, not because there is no "human nature" to count on, but because with an endless elaboration of new motive patterns and a limitless novelty of imagination there goes an increasing range of power subject to man's discretion. Forecast must always bear the condition "other things being equal," and with the one certainty that other things will not be equal.

In the broad sweep, the lines of "social evolution" lose their clarity. The eighteenth-century assurance of progress with "enlightenment" has faded—not into noth-

ing as those would hold who have progressed beyond
"progress"—but to a thin hope: we still endeavor to educate our young! There is no law that can chart the curve
of social change; and on the whole we cherish our unpre-
dictability! We listen respectfully to the prophets of
Untergang, with the reserved expectation that they will
Go Under first. And as for the rhythm of rise-and-decay
of civilizations—that stirring picture based on the valid
principle that civilization generates its own poisons is
crossed, as we have seen, by the rising level of the "unlosables." It is a refreshing change from the cult of all-
change to consider that some human achievements stay
achieved, though their significance is continually revised
by the emergence of novelty around them.

Hegel's dialectic picture of history as the March of the
Idea through the world holds up rather better than
Herbert Spencer's deduction that an industrial age must
succeed the military, and usher in peace and a tolerable
proportion of altruism. But Hegel was too wise to let his
dialectical train run to its final bumper in a German station—as he has been accused of doing—and stop there
forever; history, he judged, must move westward, and he
knew that Berlin was not the farthest west—there was still
America! More seriously, he knew that the Idea does not
stop; and he was too well aware of the infinite unfolding of
thought to use his dialectic as a frame for prophecy. He
knew the disturbing law of the supersession of truth by
truth; what we have once mastered and identified with ourselves—that we have already outpassed. Just as a psychologist who has found a "law" of human nature, and im-
prudently lets mankind know what it is, has created a
motive for defeating that particular law (tell me what my
"reactions" are, and I will give you a new one!), so an age

which should become possessed of a complete forward-looking self-consciousness would proceed to annul its validity. Neither individual man, nor man in community, will submit to be deprived of his realm of improvisation and creative prowess. This is perhaps the only "law of history" that has no exception.

There is, however, one ground of prophecy which continues to hold good: *the unreal must yield to the real.* Truth may be displaced by better truth, but never by nontruth: humanity can never give up nor go backward in its pursuit of truth at various levels. And we have fairly learned the lesson that scientific truth is not the whole of truth; this is a welcome lesson for scientists, who can no longer bear the sole responsibility for the survival of civilization: the *Bulletin of the Atomic Scientists* is their fervid ingemination of a wider citizenship. It is the quest of "reality" in which man is unreservedly engaged. Admit the multiguity of the term "reality," the principle still has a tangible meaning that the "real" will prevail over the sham. Whatever man or civilization parts company with the underlying verities of existence seals its own fate; whatever builds on them is secure. This was Carlyle's principle of forecast; he sounded the doom of shams, and we may extend his principle to whatever is specious and illusory, to the cultivation of false emotions, false arts, and false reputes, as of false securities, to the whole fabric of a culture blown up by the techniques of a venal publicity. The "Real" remains in some sense a sphinx riddle; yet we know the man and the society that sees straight and has paid in pain the price of veracity and justice. And we know the deviations from this difficult and rare realism (a realism identical with no philosophical school, but the animus of all philosophy)—on one hand the superstitions of hopeful

fancy and on the other superstitions of dogmatic negation
for which all faith is self-deceit, and all kindness hy-
pocrisy.

In brief, a valid prophecy depends on a valid metaphysic. And while a valid metaphysic is said to be hard to
arrive at, there is a chance that the principle of the
prophet of Galilee who staked his whole career on the forecast that "the kingdom of heaven is like to a grain of
mustard seed," and that in this kingdom "the weak things"
are destined "to confound the mighty," may have its
foundation in the real. The empirical mystic may be the
most genuine realist.

ii. *Decline of Superstition, Religious and Naturalist*

I FIND myself hopeful for the present and oncoming era
of mankind, because I find this kind of metaphysic in
process of growth, and the two varieties of superstition in
process of rapid decline. As the scientific spirit makes its
steady march, there is little need to quarrel one by one with
the aberrations of religious imagination; no need to list
expressly what one does *not* believe as to the miraculous
certification of divine missions. The sap of credulity ceases
to run, and the unfruitful fancies flutter to earth "like
dead leaves," while their poetic souls rise to the treasure
land of enduring myth. At the same time I find a note-
worthy decrease in the opposing type of superstition, the
dogmatic negations of a supposedly scientific world view.
Through the wide growth of logical sensitivity, the conviction that "nature is real" is far less commonly identified
with the *non sequitur* that "nothing is real but nature."
While materialism as a phase of political ideology is more
widely professed than ever before, and our humanistic

culture claims its liberty not as a will to believe but as a right to disbelieve, to be secularist, there is far less disposition to dismiss religion out of hand as a passing illusion. We have become justly chary of universal negatives.

The "naturalism" of today, strong in manifestos, treads carefully. In its wider-drawn "nature" it includes much of the beyond-nature of yesterday. It tends to consider evolution, not as a "nothing-but" primeval stuff transformed, but as an "emergence" of the undeducible: emergence could be defined as a stepwise domestication of what, in terms of the previous stage, is strictly supernatural. (I could ease the assertion a little by using the word "transcendence"; but the principle is the same!) It does not firmly shut the door on "freedom," if it is allowed to define the term. But chiefly, it agrees in the main to reject what Whitehead calls the "bifurcation of nature." It inclines to include the qualities of the world as an integral part of the total fact of "nature." This is tantamount to a new naturalism, agreeing that the night view is incomplete—in short, abstract; that nature is the union of primary with secondary, and perhaps tertiary, qualities, a vast and welcome advance in the establishment of a common philosophical groundwork.

But with the qualities, there enters into the criterion of the "real" a new factor of immense import, not yet fully accepted, but unbanishable—an aesthetic factor. This calls for special note.

iii. *Aesthetic Factor in Experience as Cognitive*

SCIENCE and philosophy alike must have their empirical foundations. The empiricism of the seventeenth century felt bound to exclude feeling in order to be mathematically objective; the empiricism of the twentieth century, while maintaining the clean objectivity of the equationable world, finds it must include feeling in order to be concrete in other phases of its world.

"Experience," once considered as a process of sense awareness, is now recognized as a process of awareness of the real, not in spite of its inescapable feeling-component but *because of it*! Experience is passion-laden, and the passion in it is not without pertinence to the nature of the world it reports. This passion may be considered a purely subjective reaction to an impassive reality. It need not be so considered. Entertain for a moment the hypothesis that the passion of human experience is not reaction alone but response, and therefore an enlargement of our empirical veracity. I am prepared to say that the experience of beauty, of awe (and it is not insignificant that for Emily Dickinson, the experience of beauty in nature was attended with what she called "awe," including a demand for her activity as interpreter [1]), like love itself, has an ontological aspect. The transformation of Eros, in Plato's view, was a movement toward reality; we begin to see the validity of that view.

This conception is strangely echoed in a fancy of Freud's later years that his "reality principle" could lead to a nonrepressive social order. Herbert Marcuse rejecting this dream (*Eros and Civilization*) proposes that the aesthetic norm may enter, between sensuousness and morality, as a guide to a free reconciliation of man and nature. I cannot join in the dream either of Freud or of Marcuse that a nonrepressive social order—if that means a nondisciplinary order—is either achievable or desirable.

---

[1] Thomas H. Johnson, *Emily Dickinson, an Interpretive Biography*, 135.

Here Plato, as in most matters, stands as the corrective to the Freudian ideal of relaxation or of costless normality. But I endorse the broad principle here coming to evidence, of an aesthetic norm which shall be, as for Schelling, an "organon" of the metaphysical real.

Hitherto, aesthetic judgments have been admitted into our ontology only by the side entrances of metaphor and symbol, while their products in poetry and art, including myth, have been considered rather as ontological play or question or at most hypothesis, not as assertion; but even as such, with an implied claim of relevance.

It is an important step in the interpretation of religion to accept this minimal claim. It places the "superstitions" of religion at once upon a plane higher than that of mere aberration. The very infinitude of art serves to illuminate the relations of the religions; for it implies a limitless variety in the expressive resources of religion, without implying confusion in its basic world view. The pertinence of the aesthetic factor, understood as explorative, becomes a path of mutual understanding rather than of discord among religions; for religion, which *is* the passion of living, must have both its identity and its variety. And it becomes a function of philosophy to find the literal basis of this unity in variety, at the point where feeling becomes ontological.

The function of philosophy in the future relations of religions thus acquires a more central vitality.

The first tendency of philosophy, as of science, is naturally enough to dwell on thought rather than feeling, to look for the general idea within the specific cult. It seeks in the several religions what is common to all, the universal within the field of faith. It proposes to relieve the

contentions of differing dogmas by discerning a Common
Denominator. And this is indeed an indispensable service,
an inductive effort resulting not alone in discovered agreement but also in simplification, and simplification is a need
increasing with the intricacy of modern types of civilization.

In this respect, the services of Vedanta have been out-
standing, especially in its more recent developments as
interpreted by the Belur Math, the Ramakrishna center
near Calcutta, which transplated into many western
centers finds itself speaking easily in terms of western
experience. This "Western Vedanta" [2] proclaims that
"authentic mystics of all religions are talking about the
same Truth, and that the central Reality can be ap-
proached from many different standpoints"; further that
"this emphasis upon the common points of all religions,
not their differences, makes an appeal to the liberal man
of the modern day." [3] It moves toward what Radhakrishnan describes as a "rational faith which does not mock the
free spirit of man, a new vision of God." [4]

But to a large extent this Western Vedanta has escaped
the tendency of the philosophical generalizer to concentrate exclusively on the intellectual elements of religion,
lighting on a few staples of doctrine—say God, Freedom,
Destiny—omitting too much, passing lightly over elements of feeling and observance. Vedanta concerns itself
with the One, but also with purpose, passion, and the quest
of peace. Our present era in philosophy has also seen more

[2] Gerald Heard in *Prabuddha Bharata*, Jan., 1950, says that "a new
thing has come into history—that is Western Vedanta . . . a living
religion and not an academic study."
[3] From *Vedanta and the West* by the Vedanta Society of Southern
California.
[4] *Recovery of Faith*, 1955.

deeply. Consider the passion-laden work of a Nietzsche, radically critical of current Christianity in the name of a transvaluation of values, itself religious in animus. Consider the flowering in our day of a "psychology of religion," essentially a concealed philosophy in revolt against emotionless discussions of religious thought.

Consider the work of such inquirers as Gerald Heard, who explores from the standpoint of a western biologist— as Ramakrishna did from the Indian standpoint—the common factors of "realization." Nor should we forget that John Dewey, in his search for the natural bases of a "Common Faith," found a place for "mystic experience" which he would perhaps prefer to call "natural piety," but which I should identify as the ontological empiricism of feeling.

In these various ways, philosophy, as interpreter of the broader empiricism, moves toward a more adequate synthesis of the essentials of the religions.

iv. *Philosophic Advance from General to Particular: Incarnation*

BUT so long as it remains in the general, even in the generalities of feeling and observance, philosophy has not yet done its chief service to the religion of the future. For religion has a special concern with the circumstance that our actual world is a particular world, and a world of particulars; and that the roots of feeling are there.

It is tempting, but not accurate, to say that nothing but particulars exists; not accurate, because particulars give existence to the generals they embody. But without particular being, nothing exists. It is a striking merit of the present age in philosophy that we feel once more the significance of plain existence; of being, in its measureless difference from nonbeing. And religion is uniquely occupied with this difference: it raises the question whether "God" may be precisely this, the ingredient of being in all beings, the "I am."

And if so, what of one's own existence? Do I exist only in the prior existence of God? Am I wholly dependent and created in my particular selfhood? Or have I, though a creature, still the power to create? For without that power, what worth can my individual existence have? These are the basic issues of life, of the meaning of life, of religion.

And if this is the case, is it not essential to religion to come to the particular, to the destiny of this particular stream of being on this petty planet, yes, to the thoughts, deeds, fortunes, of the individual souls therein engaged? Otherwise, what is prayer and what the fate of the personal soul? If God is only the Universal and Infinite, does he not become negligible to the negligible, to the personal atom lost in measureless expanse and time? Religion must somehow present itself as the personal intimacy of the Whole to the Infinitesimal, as an inversion both of the physical and of the conceptual perspectives, an inversion adumbrated by Cusanus in his strange doctrine of the coincidence of opposites, the greatest expressing itself in the least. In brief, it belongs to the general essence of all religion that at some point it escapes generality, clothes itself in particulars, descends to the shaping of personal deeds and hopes, becomes "a" religion.

If our philosophy cannot interpret this step, it fails the future at a decisive point.

Theology in various religions has, of course, long since found its way to this point. The doctrine of Incarnation could be defined as a generality whose role it is to escape from generality, accepting the responsibility of the universal for realization in the particular. The doctrine of Creation shares this responsibility: it represents the particular universe as a result of decision, a passage from idea to fact. Though the phrase "the best of all possible worlds" is now recognized, in the logic of infinite collections, as unmeaning,[5] what is created must in some sense embody a purpose. And while quite literally every decision is an incarnation, clothing an ideal desideratum in (partly irrelevant) factuality, the doctrine of Incarnation goes farther: it proposes that the One-and-Real can become and has become recognizably and personally present in particular human form or forms.

It is indeed this doctrine which most sharply divides the existing great religions, and which is least amenable to the assimilating tendencies we have considered. These religions separate not simply on the ground of a postulate of divine dignity: God "neither begets nor is begotten." They separate on the line of patent inconsistency: the Ineffable by definition cannot become visible and tangible; the Eternal cannot limit itself to a career in space and time. There can be prophets or a Prophet; there can be messiahs or a Messiah; there can be logoi or a Logos: but God-in-human-form, it is judged, must remain in the realm of fable.

There are suggestions for a solution of this dilemma in Indian speculations, having in the background their own traditions of the avatars of divine personages—speculations which culminate in the philosophy of Sankara and the contemporary Vedanta. In the conception of the world's ultimate and absolute unity, with its corollary of

[5] "Fact and Destiny," *The Review of Metaphysics*, March, 1951, 331 ff.

the unreality of individual distinctions, the identity of
each soul with the One implies that in their true essence all
men are divine. "Vedanta affirms that in his real nature
every person is divine, and that happiness and genuine
self-expression can be gained to the extent that, through
love for God and neighbor, he permits this divinity to be
manifested." [6]

Here the language of Vedanta allows itself a certain
assimilation to western tradition; but through it we recognize a specific answer to the central issue of all metaphysics
—the unity or plurality of the world, the nature of being,
the meaning of individuality. Here Vedanta approaches
tangency to Royce's profound doctrine of the one Individual from whose will all individuality proceeds. But where
all are divine, we seem to have returned to the general;
and the embodiment of the One in the many remains affected by the unreality of the many, together with that of
the empirical universe and its historical process.

The present stage of philosophical inquiry provides certain new vistas which may lead to the resolution of this
impasse.

It does so by way of a clearer understanding of selfhood
in its relation to other self and to the world; a clearer
understanding of that intersubjectivity whereby each individual in his solitude is nevertheless a participant in the
universality of his world, of its essence and its standards.
The individual is *not per se "divine"*; he participates in
the divine nature, but the degree of his participation is a
function of his liberty. He has the choice of acting as ego
atom or as contributing partner of the divine purpose.
Human individuality, while sharing in the absolute Being,

[6] *Vedanta and the West.*

and participating in the absoluteness of that Being's judgments of the actual—the universally true or false, the universally good or evil—has the double possibility of making itself solitary, monadic, mortal, or enjoying the freedom of sharing in the world purpose of the One. In the presence of the universal Thou-art, there is an immediate summons to live by objective thought (including science) and by creative action: and in so far as the individual responds, partially or completely, to this imperative, God is literally, through him, at work in history.

Through this vista of free participation,[7] the scruples of Judaism and Islam to accept a doctrine of Incarnation, which in view of the history of doctrine have genuine grounds, can cease to be barriers of separation. And at the same time, the valid insights of Vedanta can be relieved of their relative detachment from the concerns of human history.

v. *Advance beyond Empiricism in Realizing an Imputed Possibility in What a Man Is*

THE full significance of this radical freedom becomes apparent in an individual's dealing with other individuals. "Deal with men as what they are" is a rule of good morals and of good sense: *but what are they?* Here we pass beyond the scope of a pure empiricism. A person's psychoanalytical factuality is one thing, *his possibility* is something else, not discoverable by scientific observation. The question, What is he? has to be answered, *He is both*; both his actual and his possible self. Or more accurately, He is many; for his possibilities are many, for better and for worse. How, then, is he to be treated "as what he is"?

[7] *Human Nature and Its Remaking,* ch. XIV.

To "love one's neighbor" would be to deal with him, not blindly but with responsible provocation, on the basis of his favorable possibilities *as creatively discerned by you*, including therein that not actual but potential divinity which your deed may elicit. Then one understands that startling saying, "Inasmuch as ye have done it unto one of the least of these my brethren, ye have done it unto me." Since the finite self already participates to some extent in the infinite life, the true mystic finds his deity not alone at the end of the negative path, as the Absolute-that-is-not-the-finite, but also there, on the highway,

> Where move in strange democracy
> The million masks of God.

And these ministerings of man to man are not merely items of creature comfort bestowed on passing needs; they are acts of transforming this human history into the pattern of a divine community *through changing the relational scheme of its units*.

Human purpose thus acquires the sense of bringing something to pass which apart from this, our finite act, would simply not exist. It fulfills Nietzsche's rightful demand for something "beyond all your compassion." It carries out the demand that we realize our Buddha nature, and help others to realize theirs. But beyond this, it takes the shape of a creative task within a process having an affirmative and universal goal in history, even though the city to be built, already present in its conspectus—*universus hic mundus jam una civitas*—is still in its architecture out of sight. On this conception, the religions may, and will, ultimately unite.

EPILOGUE

WITH the relations between religions thus relieved of confusion, at once by the growing unity of their unlosable essences, the understanding acceptance of variety, and the quiet convergence of purpose in the identity of a historic task, religion will be able to bring a new vitality into the disturbed motivations of mankind.

It will summon man to give himself to his science without reserve and without despair, knowing that the purpose of science cannot involve the banishing of purpose from the cosmos, and that the empiricism of sense data is but a limiting edge of the widening empiricism of the ontological passions, including those of the lover, the artist, and the prophet, which open the door to reality.

It will sustain that integrity of volition which the state must assume and cannot by itself command. Each individual person, being summoned to find in the apparent disorder of human history a *telos* with which he can co-operate, and in so doing to find the worth of his own existence, will discover in his will-to-participate in a world task a nonpolitical basis for those legal rights which, taken as costless gifts of nature, work for the corruption of the political community.

It will uphold the dignity of the individual human being by upholding his responsibility. For it will leave in his hand the freedom to respond or not to respond to the call to co-operate with the divine purpose. This unique trust of freedom, vested in no other creature, marks both his nobility and his peril, his fitness to maintain and his capacity to destroy the oncoming civilization. It will assure the individual that his use of this freedom, his disposition of his own solitude, is the instant concern of the center of all Being.

It will also assure him that the way of his duty is at the same time the way of such happiness as can come from loving and being loved, from the full employment of one's powers, and from an inner peace. But it will deal with him on the basis of a profound honor: it will promise him no escape from pain and ill fortune; it will offer him the Cross —his own. Its way to happiness is the path of a will to create in love, which is inseparable from a will to create through suffering. But that will, like love itself, is touched with the light of immortality.

So far as this stern and undeluded but life-affirming will prevails among a people, the state will recover those necessary powers which in our opening study we saw slipping from its grasp—among them its power to educate, and also to punish. Let me here cite a word of Sir Winston Churchill's, all the more apposite because devoid of any reference to our present context:

> The mood and temper of the public with regard to the treatment of crime and criminals is one of the most unfailing tests of the civilization of any country. A calm, dispassionate recognition of the rights of the accused, and even of the convicted criminal against the state; a constant heart-searching by all charged with the duty of punishment; a desire and an eagerness to rehabilitate . . . ; tireless efforts toward the discovery of creative and regenerative processes; unfailing faith that there is a treasure, if you can only find it, in the heart of every man. These are the symbols which . . . mark and measure the stored-up strength of a nation . . . proof of the living virtue in it.[1]

[1] *Probation*, Dec., 1941.

The "constant heart-searching" of the punisher . . .
the "rights of the accused even against the state" . . .
"the unfailing faith that there is a treasure in the heart of
every man" . . . these do indeed represent a strength
stored up, not in a day, and not by an accumulated mass
of mental measurements, but in the long reflections of a
people upon their deeper insights of human possibility.
Clearly, these reflections are not achieved by the political
power itself; nor are they as yet universal. They can enter
the structure of law in the coming world civilization only
as a certain "spirit of the laws" first permeates its fabric.
It is a spirit which arises from a severe and resolute confidence in human nature, a confidence which refuses to
flatter by asserting fitness without effort, and which refuses to discourage by asserting limits set by circumstance,
declaring *not the achieved dignity but the potential divinity* of the individual soul.

The historical sources of that spirit remain an unfailing spring, whose potency makes and will make for the
healing of the nations.

*Opus hic terminatum
sed non consummatum
dico.*

Appendix: Humanist Vision and the Idea of God; Max Otto on the Sources of Natural Faith

THE career of religion through history has to be a constant encounter with developments in science and the demands of a changing culture. Because of this, it has also to be a constant "return to nature," i.e., to the primitive intuitions in which it is born. Every book, therefore, in which severe analysis plays a necessary part ought in the end to do penance in the effort to recover an elemental sense of the human grounds of faith.

Nothing could be more favorable to such a recovery than an open and friendly meeting between minds presumably disagreeing in outlook—let us say between theists and nontheists of the humanist persuasion. In such an encounter the theist is driven by the humanist to recover his own sources in common experience. And the humanist is driven to remind himself of something in his relation to nature akin to that of the mystic to his Ultimate Being.

It so happens that in 1932 there was such a "Conversation," published under the title *Is There a God?* There were three participants—two theists, empirical and rational, Professors Wieman and Macintosh, with Professor Max Otto of the University of Wisconsin holding the humanist view. It fell to my lot to review this book for *The Christian Century* (March 8, 1933), and as an unexpected

result to receive from Max Otto a priceless letter, so remarkable in its magnanimity and integrity of spirit that
in spite of the kindly things he says about my review I am
impelled to share it—first for what it says about *him*, his
extraordinary willingness to reconsider a firm position,
and then for the evidence it brings that what I have called
the recognition of mystic by mystic, and their *rapprochement* across apparent gulfs, are not limited to relations
between avowed faiths.

First, the review:

WHAT IF GOD IS GONE?

Is THERE A GOD? A CONVERSATION. *By Henry Nelson Wieman, Douglas Clyde Macintosh and Max Carl Otto.*

The existence of God is not an academic question: it is less
so today than at any time we can think of. To more people
than ever before, the whole problem of religion turns on this
one question. And to most of these people, the question appears
to be of the first order of seriousness, in the sense that it makes
a momentous difference which way the answer falls.

But what difference does it make? It should be easy to say,
if the question is indeed so vital. Yet it is not wholly easy; for
there is a difference between what anyone thinks God *is,* and
what God *means* to him. Many people of our generation have
quietly dropped God out of their lives—quietly but deliberately—and find they get on as well as before, perhaps better.
God had "existed" for them; but he had not "meant" anything
in particular: as a visitor with no special errand, he could go,
and leave only a sense of relief. It is just this consciously
experimental, and apparently successful, godlessness—characteristic of our time—on the part of many persons of high
character, and of at least one great state—that makes the question terribly imminent to so many others. The biographical
arguments outweigh the philosophic.

Let us find our issue, then, in this way: If there is no God, something surely is gone out of the world which we used to think was there. *What is it that is gone?*

For some, it is a great thing, but far off—a sort of supervision of the universe that never comes close home. To believe in God, for such persons, means chiefly a sense that the total drift of things is being looked after, as by a competent and trustworthy overseer, who really knows more about it than we do and who has the fundamental interests of mankind at heart; so that one is free to concentrate on human business, without useless worry over the cosmos. It is interesting that this freedom of mind to be whole-heartedly human, assuming all the responsibilities one can do anything about, is very much the effect that Mr. Otto desires to achieve by getting rid of God! For the persons we are now speaking of, the loss of God would leave them ill at ease about the framework of human life; a vast responsibility would have fallen on them which they can neither shake off nor discharge. They could school themselves to forget it and be all the more neighborly the while. But they would secretly know that we human beings are cultivating a garden in the midst of a desert which in all likelihood will eventually cover both garden and gardeners; while it, the desert, will never know what it has done. We shall do our best while we are here together—that is not futile; it is only that the name of the whole picture is Futility. That, I think, is a real difference.

To others the loss of God would mean the loss of something very intimate. William James once tried to express it, if my memory is not at fault, as a kind of quiet music playing in the back of the mind. That is not very definite; but one understands how, when music stops, existence abruptly "comes to earth"—provided one has been enjoying the music! "Companionship" would have been too personal and shapely a word for William James; the vague elevation of music was nearer his sense of the divine as a factor in consciousness or subconsciousness. But the music is *addressed* to the mind it inhabits, and to many this presence takes companionly form, without any of the palpable intrusions of human comradeship. It means, at least, "He is there"; and because of this, my solitude

can never be deserted and insignificant. This inward presence
of God is a continual invitation to greatness in what is intrinsically small, a reminder of the unlimited possibility of the
limited human person, a dignifying of the commonplace, a
music?—yes, but a magical music into which one can feed the
disharmonies of plain living and hear them blended into a
strange, unbelievable grandeur of silent sound. The outer
world has its own unremitting summons to heroic action; the
inner presence of God has tempted souls here and there into
retreat from these outer demands, and then they have lost that
presence; its true function is not to compete with the outer
claims and interests (as Mr. Otto fears), but rather to abet
them by raising the soul to the level of the greatest external
demand. To lose God would leave the human self measuring its
sole strength against the tasks of history—a Bruno or a Joan
of Arc alone before the powers and the fagots. It seemed to
them that they were not alone. For the pure love of man or of
justice, others have done as much. Yet there is here also, I
think, a real difference.

At the lowest terms, is the issue not something like this—
whether the world we live in *has or has not a meaning?* If it
has, then the meaning of the whole may invade the part, and
our individual lives may also have a meaning? If it has not, its
meaninglessness infects us also, and all our doings; unless we
decline to think. And if the world as a whole has a meaning,
there is one who entertains that meaning, there is God.

I find it easy to understand how men may come to doubt
the existence of God. I find it less easy to understand how the
value of God can be doubted, if he exists. I surmise that Mr.
Otto's difficulty is that he looks too narrowly for that value; he
misses it because it is too obvious and pervasive. The word God
is short and thuddy; it suggests a finite knob of existence
somewhere, doing finite things. These finite things necessarily
intrude upon and displace other finite things; and Mr. Otto
finds it desirable that they should be ruled out of the reckon-
ing, and we men left squarely to our own devices, which, he
believes (with a sanguineness, I suspect, *not* born of experience) will be found sufficient. He reads history as the steady
displacement of the work of this interfering God—as it largely

is—and looks to the inevitable end of the series of subtractions from any finite quantity. I find myself much in accord with Mr. Otto's feeling about divine intrusions. I see why he is bothered when Mr. Wieman singles out a phase of the social order, a perfectly genuine phase, and calls it God. Whatever is a process among other processes, a finite factor in the living mesh of being, may have strong analogies with the divine life; but unless it casts its redeeming quality into the whole of things, or derives it therefrom, it falls short of what we mean by God. But Mr. Otto seems to me to overlook the comprehensive and therefore *non-intrusive* work of God, as the source of meaning in the whole sum of things, and hence in the motives of the soul.

And on this account he appears mistaken in supposing that the extension of human sway over the former domain of the finite works of God has involved a displacement of the center of the meaning of God. As I read history, it seems to me that we feel today much more akin to our primitive ancestors in religion than we used to; and one of my queries of the two theistic conversers is, why it is, with all their faith in experience as a source of instruction, they have made so little use of those strands of religious experience which unite sophisticated modernity with its original sources. For those who first conceived God or the divine were not wholly off the target. And while the early intuitions of the race, continually reborn, have no authoritative value, neither are they to be ignored; they restore our sense of proportion, and the major things stand out clear. Given the indispensable critical sense, determined, in Mr. Wieman's vigorous words, to "extricate the existence of God from all the crudity, fallibility, and folly of our beliefs about God," we can with the more assurance gain from elemental belief its endless instruction.

Especially to one who finds God evanescent, and the idea of God baffling, there is perennial cause of wonder in the ease with which simple folk and children get the idea of God; and hardly less in the fact that the idea they get has almost nothing in common with the pictorial caricatures usually attributed to the infant mind. Here, for example, are some low-caste Indians, boatmen of Bengal, illiterate and untutored except by way of certain traditional songs. These boatmen, setting their sails before sunrise to catch the early wind, sing—or used to sing:

> I am a lamp afloat on the water;
> At what *ghat* didst Thou set me afloat? . . .
> O Friend, End of all endless movement,
> How many bends of the river are still before me?
> And with what call wilt Thou reveal thyself to me?
> Thou wilt take me from the water,
> And there, under the protection of thy arm,
> Wilt extinguish the burning of the whole long journey!

Where, in this sensitive and intimate feeling of a Thou in the world, does one find a trace of those silly anthropomorphisms so glibly attributed to the simple of the world in their thoughts of God? There is imagery here; but the singer knows it for what it is, and the symbols drop off from the living center of his conception. What is that center? The ultimate power of the world, in the attitude of solicitous individual care for his own creatures. God is good, as love is good; and in that goodness admonishing to righteousness and devotion. But there is here no weight of correcting and chastening holiness.

The picture is unfinished on the ethical side. Listen, then, to the voice of another primitive spirit. After quoting the words of the prophet, "The voice of him that crieth in the wilderness, prepare ye the way of the lord," Karl Barth says, "This is the voice of *our conscience,* telling us of the righteousness of God. . . . What it tells is no question, no riddle, no problem, but a fact—the deepest, innermost, surest fact of life: God is righteous." I say this is the utterance of a primitive, intuitive therefore dogmatic, streak in Barth; a perception of the original mystic in him, before he had been wholly persuaded by that gnarled, intricate and unhappy philosophic genius, Kierkegaard, to distrust his own direct insight into the truth of things.

Such utterances, whether of the Bengalese baül or of the Swiss pastor-theologian, are not, of course, to be accepted merely because they come out of a brave soul's volcanic inner certitude, somehow continuous with the inner lava of the world.

But they do put *theses* before us, invite corroboration or rejection from our own inner voices, compel review of our sources of knowledge, and remind us, in the midst of our reasonings, what the word God has meant to the race.

God has meant responsible creative power, individual solicitude, the dominance of moral law over every other law of human destiny—the complete rebuke of the pretense of natural immensities to be supreme in their enveloping indifference. God means, not a partial inner aspect of nature, but the thoroughgoing subordination of nature to a greater, albeit non-intrusive, spiritual power. To say God is "All" or that he is "Absolute" or "Infinite" might be accurate—I think so—but it would be philosophic language, and immediately excite diverting difficulties in the obdurate philosophic mind. But at least in all the sturdy common thoughts of God he has been *commensurate with the cosmos*; throwing the physical universe as well as the world of men into the relation of dependence. And at the same time this supreme reality is capable of *personal nearness*. God is the embodied paradoxical union of the vast and the intimate. The word Spirit conveys this paradox.

Does any such Being exist? If not, I am ready to say with Mr. Otto there is no God. Though I wholly acknowledge the right of redefinition, I would not wish to apply the word to a lesser entity: I would stand with Mr. Macintosh in preferring to put the existence of God into question rather than avoid that question by moderating the significance of his being.

And I would agree with Mr. Otto that to any one who accepts "Nature" as the comprehensive name for the world, and who judges its hypothetical dispositions toward men by the impressions of human fortune, the God we have indicated, who in some sense denies the pretenses of Nature, is simply impossible. When for the sake of the argument Mr. Otto entertains a conception of God, it is a sort of dramatization of the ways of the physical universe, a "transference of manlike characteristics to cosmological nature." From such a "great Cosmic Power" there is, indeed, no reason to expect good rather than evil. And he is right also, I believe, in judging that the case is not improved by conceiving the substance of Nature as the thought of a divine mathematician.

Only, God has never meant to common humanity the mere inner animation of the natural machine. God has meant an inner life of Nature, but also so much a mastering supplement of Nature that appearances may be reversed, and physical death itself the prelude of further life. The speculations growing out of physical science are intensely relevant, but they are the mere beginning of the task. Their chief yield, so far, as Mr. Macintosh well points out (page 59), is that some of the old caveats against faith have been withdrawn, and that in some quarters it is possible to see how physical processes may be informed by thought and purpose without ceasing to be truly physical in behavior. So far, there is the mere fringe of God, a possibility of God; one may have all this and not have God.

Mr. Whitehead's God, referred to by Mr. Macintosh, has in his conception much more of the true measure of the primitive idea. Whitehead's bold and wide-reaching speculative structure shows the way thought must go to reach adequacy. He is radically dissatisfied with that pure-mathematical conception of Nature, somewhat violently thrusts back into Nature the *qualities* of experience—the stone which the quantitative builders rejected—and then calls on a God-process, distinct from the causal process, to weave these qualities, as "eternal entities," into the pattern of events. God decorates the iron trellis of causality with his roses; but power still lies with the quantitative thrust of cause and effect; and this finite deity is still less than what God has meant to men. It is an "approach," a magnificent approach; not yet an arrival.

But after all, is this not the business of thought—to approach God, not to prove him? What can we expect of experience, external experience, well mulled over, except adumbrations of God, intimations of immortality? Mr. Otto is right in saying, These are not God. But he is wrong in saying, These are not *signs of God* or even, moments of God's being. Is this not what Mr. Wieman has: an approach to God, and one of the most necessary and important of all approaches, through social experience? What he has—so long as he draws no line around it, saying This is all—does not negate the rest of God's being.

"God is much more," says Mr. Wieman, "than what I say about him."

The exhilarating feature of the present moment is that men are thinking new thoughts about God, because they are approaching him from different quarters, through various avenues of experience. That this comes about by premature despair of the way of thought is of little consequence: the two halves of the complete method will meet, as they do in Mr. Macintosh's argument. The important thing is that overt experience is the way of renewal and novelty in our grasp of the eternal. This is eminently true of Mr. Wieman's thought.

My present impression is that Mr. Wieman's God is rather badly put together. He is composed of a process, having a distinctive pattern, as promoting mutuality—a process of interaction, hence presupposing interacting elements—and a set of possibilities, not visibly attached to anything. My personal feeling is—and I am sensible of very imperfect mastery of the conception—that if we hold to Mr. Wieman's ideal that God shall be knowable as other things are knowable, these possibilities can only exist as they are contemplated by some mind. And if we are to bring a mind into the picture, the process which is making for mutuality would better be brought *into the same mind,* where it could work intentionally, and not live in the uncomfortable limbo of interaction between entities that might separate and leave it wandering in the universe like a lost soul.

I surmise that Mr. Wieman's whole argument would profit if he could organize the working elements of his divine being within the focus of a self. But I greatly respect his indisposition to capitulate to the ambiguous word "personality." He was accused in one of the early papers of balancing between personality and impersonality like a tight-rope walker, an accusation which was later withdrawn. But I would venture to revive it as an element of praise. Our notions of personality are so restricted that they need always to be corrected by the notions of impersonal law, thinking of God as the moral order of the universe; and impersonal law, in turn, needs correction by personality. I believe that there is a true notion of personality

which will include them both. But meantime, if Mr. Wieman
uses now one and now the other element, he is but exemplifying
by the routes of a nobly candid empiricism that dialectical
character of our predicates of God, so much in evidence in the
thought of Kierkegaard, Barth and Brunner.

And agreeing as I do with Mr. Otto that he has no God in
the proper sense of the word, I should like to convince him that
he, too, has an approach to one. His feeling of oneness with
the endless procession of living forms, and of community with
the friendly all-sustaining earth, wherein the human spirit is
lifted above pettiness and distraction; at the same time chas-
tened by the true grandeur of the uncomprehended which
remains forever the undisclosed secret of the world—I would
not spoil the splendid integrity of this mood by trying to draw
it into another frame. But I believe most earnestly that community is the right word, and spells a relation of kind with
kind. I will not attribute even a subconscious God to Mr. Otto;
but I will say that I come under the spell of his feeling, and in
so doing touch the near edge of what I call God.

To me the answer to the question, Is there a God? is also a
matter of experience, but of the simple and primitive sort. It is
not the projection of deepest wants on distant clouds; for it is
the very meaning of objectivity. It is God that gives Nature its
secure character as something other than my private vision.
Deeper than my interaction with human fellows, which is occasional, is my interaction with Nature, which is continual: and
in interacting with it, I am being acted upon, am being made.
By what? By whatever can make a self; by my Other Self,
inalienably present. The wide reaches of the universe are
drawn together in this knot, at the focus of self-consciousness;
and as I find myself, so I find therewith an immediate sense
of God. God is the heart of Fact; and with this primary Fact
appears my first Duty, to come out of my subjectivity and
converse with him.

This is the merest beginning of the knowledge of God, far
less than that expressed by the Bengal singers or by Barth's
reading of conscience; but it has in it the germ, the primitive
affirmation, upon which further experimental knowledge can
grow. To this center, all the various "approaches" bring their

contributions; on it build the visions of the prophets and the mediators.

With it also mingles in the course of history an abundance of human error and subjective illusion. And when I think how the secret fears of good men still make of God, now and then, an unapproachable mystery, a moral tyrant or a vindictive legalist, and how, mistaking for loyalty their timorous subjection to these dour dreams, they still impose their mood, through policies of exaction and exclusion, upon many of their kind, I am at moments tempted to feel that Mr. Otto, if not quite right, may be nearer right than any of us.

But of course he is not! For the alternative is not as we made it. It is not a choice between a bad God, spoiled by subjective complexes, and no God at all. It is a choice between an imperfect God and the true God—between a God who *is* the shadow of our infirmities, cast on the clouds of the nether deep, and the God whose voice is the speech of the world's hope. I take heart to believe that after the earthquake and the fire, and the just negations that follow, "God is not in them" —there will be widely heard the still, small voice.

The University of Wisconsin
Madison

Department of Philosophy
191 Bascom Hall

April 4, 1933

Dear Professor Hocking:

For nearly a month I have hesitated to write to you about your critical review in The Christian Century, of the book *Is There a God?* I wanted my enthusiasm to cool down somewhat. The earlier impression, however, persists. I have just now once more reread the review, and its virtues, previously appreciated, still work upon me. There seems to be no good reason for waiting any longer.

It is not my purpose to discuss any differences with you, or indeed to refer to any issue or issues. In the matter of that there is but one part of your criticism which I incline to reject outright, and that has to do with another, not myself. For the rest, agree or disagree, you impel me to further observation and study, to meditation—and I had almost said prayer. The facts adumbrated are very rich and I have no doubt that I shall hereafter find myself, because of what you have said, more deeply involved in the problem than heretofore.

What remained and remains most graphically present in my mind is the way the review was done—the fairness of statement, the completely adequate understanding of the conflict, the warmth and color of the statement itself. In this art of uniting material and form in writing—surely one of the most difficult arts—you presented, so it seems to me, an example in this paper which is not often achieved even when the undertaking is far more important than any review of a book could be. Some of your sentences are so weighted and at the same time poetic, that I have repeated them for other ears as well as my own. One cannot tell: I may yet end by becoming so familiar and enamoured with the sheer rhythm of them as to feel that I understand what is meant by "the God whose voice is the speech of the world's hope." Stranger things have happened in philosophy.

Well, feeling stimulated by your thought and inwardly warmed by your style, you will forgive me, I hope, for saying so as frankly as I have.

Very sincerely yours,
(signed) M. C. OTTO.

INDEX

science, 8, 41, 50, 55, 58, 61,
   62, 65, 74, 97, 103, 146,
   148, 158, 161, 173, 174,
   183, 185
   as critic, 83, 159, 161
   of man, 56, 62
   purpose of, 61, 185
   unscientific, 62, 63, 70, 174
Secularism, 3, 44, 53, 66, 71,
   150, 175
secularization, 63
seeing, 96 f., 98, 101, 107, 113,
   134
self
   actual and possible, 183
   assertion, 91, 97
   awareness, 38 ff.
   fulfillment, 40
   transcendence, 34, 34 n., 91
   see also ego, I-think, subjec-
      tivity
sense data, 40, 70
Sermon on the Mount, 89,
   94
sex mores, 131, 131 n.
Shinto, 81, 120 n., 152
sick-soul, 104
signs, 35
Simmel, G., 34 n.,
simplicity, 85, 125, 134, 135,
   145, 161
sin, sinners, 81, 103–6, 144,
   163
   auspicious, 106 n.
skepticism, 97
slave morality, 89 n.
social gospel, 129, 133
social need, 43 f.
social science, sociology, 31, 48,
   56, 159, 161
social suffocation, 77; *see also*
   masses
Socrates, 144, 160

solipsism, 22, 25 ff., 30 ff., 33 f.,
   41, 72 n.
solitude, 31, 35, 73, 75, 107
   universality, 21 f., 107
sovereignty, 46 f.
Soviets, 12, 54, 54 n.
Spencer, Herbert, 172
Spinoza, 56, 69, 144
Spirit, 195
spiritual iron, 162–68
standards, 29, 84
state, 4, 8, 43, 45, 186
   and individual, 1 n.
   sovereignty, 45 f.
Steere, Douglas, 135
Stoic, -ism, 29, 93 n., 123
struggle for existence, 91
Subjectivism, -ity, 19, 21 f., 25,
   30 ff., 56, 71, 72 n., 74
suffering, 87 n., 94, 96, 163
substance, 19
supernature, -al, 66, 85, 96,
   103, 163, 175
superstition, 83, 85, 157, 169,
   177
symbol, 114, 124, 177
Syncretism, 146
system rejected, 76

Tagore, R., 139
Takagi, Yasaka, 119
Tao, -ism, 46, 88, 97, 143
task (mission, mandate), 95,
   119, 144, 184
technology, 45, 49, 51, 65, 77
telos, 32, 62, 102, 185
Tenrikyo, 81
tension, 125
Tertullian, 126, 160, 163 n.
theism, theist, 189
theology, 114, 180
thinking, as purposive effort,
   40

p 108 = a creed, a code, a deed+

105 = son to call men sinners

95 X n ethre = a most unlikely world view

106 = Perfection